Donated by : Michael P. McHugh

HEREDITAS
A Book of Medieval Latin Prose

HEREDITAS

A Book of Medieval Latin Prose

compiled by

S. Morris B.A. M.Ed.
Lecturer in Education, University of Birmingham

and

E. O. Furber M.A.
Senior Classics Master, Pate's Grammar School, Cheltenham

GEORGE G. HARRAP & CO. LTD
London   Toronto   Wellington   Sydney

First published in Great Britain 1970
by George G. Harrap & Co. Ltd
182-184 High Holborn, London, W.C.1

© *S. Morris and E. O. Furber* 1970

SBN   245   50317   X

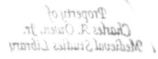
*Composed in Ehrhardt type and printed
by Alden & Mowbray Ltd at the Alden Press, Oxford
Made in Great Britain*

Preface

Our aim in presenting this collection of texts has been to make accessible to Latin teachers and students a wider range of late and medieval Latin than is at present available in annotated editions suitable for school use.

The texts, which are united by the general theme of the development of the Church, consist of selections from the works quoted. Spelling has been brought into line with Classical practice; but no other changes have been made to the original texts, except for the very occasional omission of a difficult phrase or sentence.

The texts range in difficulty of vocabulary, syntax, and style from the very simple to the standard found in Classical Latin in straightforward Caesar or Cicero. Sections 1 and 5 are simple in vocabulary, syntax, and style; sections 6 and 7 are still simple but with wider vocabulary; sections 2, 3, 4, 8, and 9 make greater demands and so have been given more generous notes.

We hope that the book will be used as a reader after about two or three years of Latin, and that it may prove suitable as a prescribed text for "O" level Latin.

S.M.
E.O.F.

Contents

Illustrations

Introduction

The authors represented in this selection span a period of more than a thousand years, and the purpose of this introduction is to show why Latin continued to be used for so long after the fall of Rome, to indicate the importance of Latin in the pattern of European history, and to place these particular authors in their appropriate setting.

Pre-medieval Europe

For many people Latin is simply the language used by the Romans in antiquity; they forget that the Roman Empire extended from Hadrian's Wall to the Sahara Desert, from the Pillars of Hercules to the Euphrates, and that in the western part of this empire Latin was the common language. It is true that the invasions of the Goths and the Vandals in the fifth century A.D. put an end to the political power of Rome, but Latin did not perish: its literature was used as a means of education, and the language itself served as a means of communication for all educated Europeans. Rome left us a Hereditas—a true inheritance which was the means of saving civilization and a continuing source of inspiration for educated men.

It was, however, for only a minority that a formal education was available. For the rest, the Latin which had been spoken in Western Europe developed into the languages which we now call Romance languages. Even at the height of Roman power the spoken Latin of the common people of Gaul, Spain, and Italy had differed from the literary Latin of Cicero and Caesar, while in Britain, one of the last areas to come under Roman power, Latin was probably little used outside the urban areas. When Rome fell and invading tribes mingled with the original inhabitants the common tongues gradually changed: case-endings disappeared and pronunciation altered, so that by A.D. 800 the vernacular tongues could no longer be called Latin, and Latin itself was unintelligible to the common people.

Its survival was due entirely to the Christian Church. The Emperor Constantine had proclaimed toleration for the Christians in A.D. 313, and in A.D. 394 all other religions were forbidden. The Roman world was divided into bishoprics and in A.D. 385 Jerome produced an authoritative translation of the Bible into Latin, for this was naturally the language of all Christian worship in Western Europe. In the troubled times of the invasions bishops such as Augustine of Hippo, in North Africa, spoke for the Church. The invaders took over Rome's military and political power, but central authority was lost; in the turmoil men looked to the Church as the centre of moral authority, culture, and learning. As the vernacular languages developed and the barbarians themselves were converted to Christianity, so the Church was faced with a problem of communication: the vast majority of these new generations of Christians had no knowledge of Latin, yet Latin was the language of worship and the Bible in the West. It was therefore essential that priests and monks, drawn from the communities that they were going to serve and able to communicate in the vernacular tongues, should be trained in Latin; if Christianity was to survive as a world faith, then schools and monasteries for training the priesthood were essential.

It was in Ireland that the problem had first to be faced, for Latin had been virtually unknown there. During the fifth and sixth centuries many monasteries, such as Clonard and Kells, were founded, and the Irish monks were such enthusiastic travellers and missionaries that they then proceeded to organize the training of English clergy at schools such as Lindisfarne. These Anglo-Saxon schools in their turn became so famous that Western Europe turned to them for assistance. The schools at Jarrow and York successively had the highest reputations—Jarrow, where Bede (673–735) not only served as a monk and wrote the *Ecclesiastical History*, but also developed his great talent as a teacher. The fame of the school at York was assured by the presence of Alcuin (732–804) as its master.

Meanwhile on the Continent the Franks had created a powerful state. They had conquered the whole of France, and Charlemagne (742–814) extended his power over Northern Spain, Western Germany, Bohemia, Switzerland, and Northern Italy. It was to the Church that he looked for the provision of educated laymen who would help in the administration of his realm. In 782 he persuaded Alcuin to leave York and accept the headship of the Palace School in his capital, Aix-la-Chapelle. Many other schools in the monasteries of France and Germany were to develop along the lines instituted by Alcuin, and the survival of a Latin-speaking Church was assured.

The Medieval World

The educational aims and achievements of the eighth and ninth centuries had been mainly concerned with the teaching of the Latin language itself for ecclesiastic and administrative purposes. Creative work, such as Einhard's *Life of Charlemagne*, was comparatively rare. With the development of the feudal system, life became much more settled: farming was more profitable, trade increased, markets became necessary, larger urban communities grew up around them. These social changes encouraged men to look at Latin writers with a fresh purpose. Prosperous citizens and communities, eager to organize the rule of law and stable government, now looked at Latin writers to rediscover the knowledge which had been acquired in antiquity and since forgotten. In particular they were concerned with law, science, medicine, and philosophy. Although Greek was almost unknown, much of the work of Aristotle, Galen, and other Greek scientists was translated into Latin from the Arabic versions current in the Islamic part of Spain.

The medieval schools devoted their attention not so much to the elements of Latin as to those authors which provided a training in rhetoric, law, medicine, and literary studies. They served professional rather than religious aims. Very often monks and priests were drawn away from religious life to that of the Court; for the increased prosperity of Europe brought a more luxurious style of life for the wealthy, and a powerful prince often summoned men who had distinguished themselves in learning to assist him in his government and to exercise their literary skill in praise of their patron. Latin was now in constant use in administration (*e.g.*, Domesday Book), in recording laws, in the dispensation of charters, and in the recording of history as in the work of William of Malmesbury, who continued the history of English kings from the point at which Bede had stopped.

This increase in prosperity was linked also with the Crusades. These expeditions, which took place at intervals during the twelfth and thirteenth centuries, turned men's attention away from Northern Europe and focused it once again on the Mediterranean area. Europeans came into close contact with the Islamic and Byzantine world; the journeys of William de Rubruquis (1253) and of the Polo family are indications of men's interest in the Eastern world.

The Renaissance

It was the Italian city-states such as Genoa, Venice, and

Pisa that were most closely involved with the new trade routes to the East; they were also quicker to make the transition from feudalism than larger units like France and England. It is therefore not surprising that the spirit of the Renaissance was apparent first in Italy. The scholars of medieval times had been concerned with rediscovering the practical information contained in the literature of Greece and Rome; they had also been anxious to harmonize this knowledge with Christian ideals and theology. At the end of the fourteenth century there was a change in men's attitude to the classics: Petrarch and his successors in Italy were interested much more in the underlying spirit of antiquity, when men were not concerned about personal salvation, but were interested in man for man's sake alone—this attitude came to be called Humanism.

Towards the end of the fifteenth century the impact of these new ideas was felt in Northern Europe: Greek had now taken its place by the side of Latin, and the invention of printing had made books much more readily available. But in Northern Europe Humanism was not regarded as an alternative to Christianity; there were many scholars who felt that a proper study of antiquity, together with a study of the Bible in its original languages, would revitalize Christianity and purge its doctrine of much obscurity and error. The most prominent figure in English Humanism was Thomas More (1478–1535), a devout Catholic and a brilliant lawyer and politician; he is best remembered for his *Utopia*, first written in Latin, then translated into many languages, which showed an ideal city where the ideals of Christianity were logically developed in the social and political system.

Contemporary with Thomas More was Erasmus (1466–1536), a Dutchman who dominated the intellectual life of Northern Europe. His works were best-sellers, and his purpose was to bring about a reformation of the Church from within. Erasmus argued that all the greatest Christian Fathers had derived much of their learning from the classics, and he advocated a wise use of classical authors as the foundation for the education of a Christian. In addition to his didactic works, we have a great mass of Latin correspondence between Erasmus and his contemporaries, showing how Latin was a common means of communication between men of different nationalities.

It was not only the theologians who used Latin to publish their views. The sixteenth and seventeenth centuries saw advances in many fields of science, and the scientists often used Latin in publishing their discoveries, so that they might reach fellow-scientists in other countries. One of the earliest was Vesalius, who published his work on anatomy (*De Fabrica Humani Corporis*) in 1543. Copernicus (1543) and Galileo (1610), in defiance of the Catholic Church, published fundamentally new theories of the universe. Gilbert published his *De Magnete* in 1600, Harvey his *De Motu Cordis* in 1628.

Latin was still being used by scientists such as Galvani and Linnaeus in the eighteenth century, but as a means of universal communication it was now plainly on the decline. In some countries the Reformation had resulted in Latin being associated with Popery; the vernacular languages had now reached a state of stability: translations of the Bible were now available in them, and they had established their own right to be used as a medium for literature. Today the most important practical use of Latin is the universally recognized system of naming plants and animals, but no-one who is interested in the development of any aspect of European thought can afford to ignore the part that Latin has played in preserving for us the civilizations of Greece and Rome, which are still a constant source of inspiration to those who study their achievements.

Introductory Notes on Medieval Syntax Usages

The following notes refer to frequently found variations from the grammar and syntax of Classical Latin. All examples are taken from the selected texts.

1. Case Usages

(a) Ablative to express duration of time:

Cumque praefatus clericus aliquot diebus apud eum hospitaretur . . . (3, 8)

When the priest was staying with him for several days . . .

(b) Accusative with *permitto*:

quoad eum valetudo permiserat . . . (6, 121)

as far as his health allowed him . . .

2. Quod, quia, quoniam introducing reported statements

(a) With the indicative:

cognovimus quia Melita insula vocabatur. (1, 88)

we found out that the island was called Malta.

(b) With the subjunctive:

Et per illam perticam potest cognosci quod domus illa sit templum Idolorum. (7, 154)

And by that pole it can be seen that that house is the temple of the idols.

3. Indicative in Reported Questions

Panes vero . . . nobis ignotum est ubi praeparantur. (5, 59)
To be sure we do not know where the loaves are baked.

4. Infinitive in Reported Commands

suadeo vobis bono animo esse. (1, 44)
I urge you to be of good cheer.
rogabat Paulus omnes sumere cibum. (1, 62)
Paul asked them all to take food.

5. Subjunctive

(*a*) With *quamquam*, *antequam*, *postquam*, with no special
meaning:
Quamquam cervix obesa . . . videretur . . . (6, 47)
Although his neck seemed fat . . .

(*b*) With *cum*, meaning "when", in primary sequence:
*Et tunc cum sit dies festus . . . ipsi extrahunt praedictas
imagines.* (7, 205)
And then, when it is a feast day . . . they themselves drag
out the aforesaid idols.

(*c*) With *dum*, meaning "when":
Dum autem perfinissent debitum vespertinale . . . (5, 90)
And when they had finished their evening duty . . .

6. Gerundive where Classical Latin would have a present participle

Et spargit ter ad meridiem, qualibet vice flectendo genu. (7,
99)
And he sprinkles [it] thrice to the south, on each occasion
bending the knee.

7. Double compound tenses

Quando ergo ingressus fui praedictam idolatriam . . . (7, 156)
When therefore I entered the aforesaid temple of the idols.
postquam ingressus fueram templum . . . (7, 172)
after I had entered the temple . . .

16

1. St Paul's Voyage to Rome

Christianity was born at a very favourable moment in history. The conquests of Alexander the Great had spread Greek culture and the Greek language far beyond the coastlands of the Eastern Mediterranean; wherever the early Christian missionary went he could be sure that he would be understood. Later, as the Church spread westwards, it became necessary for the scriptures to be translated into Latin for use in Italy, Gaul, Spain, Africa, and Britain. There was certainly a Latin Bible soon after A.D. 200, but the authoritative version, still in use in the Roman Catholic Church, was the translation made by Jerome, leader of a community of monks at Bethlehem, between A.D. 390 and 405.

The journeys of the missionaries were also made much easier by the security provided by the Roman Empire: the Pax Romana ensured the rule of law throughout the world; brigandage and piracy were rare; travel was made quicker and safer by the Roman system of roads. There were no customs officials at the frontiers, no passport regulations, no currency restrictions. The possession of Roman citizenship was of great value; on several occasions it was a means of protection for Paul against the bitter opposition of the Jews; their hostility was so strong that eventually he exercised his right of appeal to the Emperor.

The last two chapters of the Acts of the Apostles describe Paul's eventful voyage to Rome under escort; we do not know

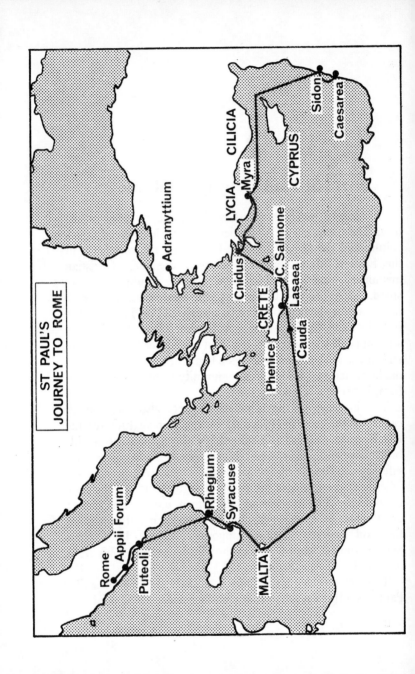

ST PAUL'S
JOURNEY TO ROME

Rome
Appii Forum
Puteoli
Rhegium
Syracuse
MALTA
Cauda
CRETE
Phenice
Lasaea
C. Salmone
Cnidus
Myra
LYCIA
CILICIA
CYPRUS
Sidon
Caesarea
Adramyttium

the exact year, but it was probably about A.D. 60. There was already a Christian community in Rome, and it met him and escorted him on the last few miles of his journey; four years later this community was sufficiently numerous for Nero to make them the scapegoats for the great fire of Rome.

———

Paul, under escort, begins the journey to Rome in a coasting vessel. He is transferred to a larger ship and reaches Crete at the end of the sailing season.

Ut autem iudicatum est navigare eum in Italiam, tradiderunt Paulum cum reliquis custodiis centurioni nomine Iulio cohortis Augustae. Ascendentes navem Adrumetinam, incipientem navigare circa Asiae loca sustulimus, perseverante nobiscum Aristarcho Macedone Thessalonicensi. Sequenti 5 autem die devenimus Sidonem; humane autem tractans Iulius Paulum, permisit ad amicos ire, et curam sui agere. Et inde cum sustulissemus, subnavigavimus Cyprum, propterea quod essent venti contrarii. Et pelagus Ciliciae et Pamphiliae navigantes venimus Myram quae est Lyciae. Et 10 ibi inveniens centurio navem Alexandrinam navigantem in Italiam, transposuit nos in eam.

Et cum multis diebus tarde navigaremus, et vix devenissemus contra Cnidum, prohibente nos vento, adnavigavimus Cretae, iuxta Salmonem. Et vix iuxta navigantes venimus in 15 locum quendam qui vocatur Boniportus, cui iuxta erat civitas Lasaea.

Against Paul's advice they set sail again, but are caught in a storm.

Multo autem tempore peracto, et cum iam non esset tuta navigatio eo quod et ieiunium praeteriisset, consolabatur eos Paulus dicens eis: "Viri, video quoniam cum iniuria et multo 20 damno non solum oneris et navis, sed etiam animarum nostrarum, incipit esse navigatio." Centurio autem gubernatori et nauclero magis credebat quam his quae a Paulo dicebantur et cum aptus portus non esset ad hiemandum, plurimi statuerunt consilium navigare inde, si quomodo possent devenientes Phoenicem hiemare, portum Cretae respicientem ad africum et ad corum.

Adspirante autem austro, aestimantes propositum se tenere, cum sustulissent legebant Cretam. Non post multum autem misit se contra ipsam ventus typhonicus, qui vocatur euro-aquilo; cumque arrepta esset navis, et non posset conari in ventum, data nave flatibus ferebamur. In insulam autem quandam decurrentes, quae vocatur Cauda, potuimus vix obtinere scapham. Qua sublata adiutoriis utebantur, accin-gentes navem, timentes ne in Syrtim inciderent; summisso vase sic ferebantur. Valida autem nobis tempestate iactatis, sequenti die iactum fecerunt; et tertia die suis manibus armamenta navis proiecerunt. Neque autem sole neque sideribus apparentibus per plures dies, et tempestate non exigua imminente, iam ablata erat spes omnis salutis nostrae.

Paul reassures his fellow-passengers. Nearing land, the crew unsuccessfully attempt to abandon ship.

Et cum multa ieiunatio fuisset, tunc stans Paulus in medio eorum dixit: "Oportebat quidem, viri, audito me non tollere a Creta, lucrique facere iniuriam hanc et iacturam; et nunc suadeo vobis bono animo esse, amissio enim nullius animae erit ex vobis praeterquam navis. Adstitit enim mihi hac nocte angelus Dei cuius sum ego et cui deservio, dicens, 'Ne timeas, Paule; Caesari te oportet adsistere, et ecce donavit tibi Deus omnes qui navigant tecum.' Propter quod bono animo estote, viri; credo enim Deo quia sic erit quemadmodum dictum est mihi. In insulam autem quandam oportet nos devenire."

Sed posteaquam quartadecima nox supervenit, navigantibus nobis in Adria, circa mediam noctem, suspicabantur nautae apparere sibi aliquam regionem. Qui et summittentes bolidem invenerunt passus viginti; et pusillum inde separati invenerunt passus quindecim. Timentes autem ne in aspera loca incideremus, de puppi mittentes ancoras quattuor, optabant diem fieri. Nautis vero quaerentibus fugere de navi, cum misissent scapham in mare sub obtentu quasi inciperent a prora ancoras extendere, dixit Paulus centurioni et militibus: "Nisi hi in nave manserint, vos salvi fieri non potestis." Tunc absciderunt milites funes scaphae, et passi sunt eam excidere.

They run the ship aground, and all reach the shore safely.

Et cum lux inciperet fieri, rogabat Paulus omnes sumere cibum, dicens: "Quartadecima die hodie exspectantes ieiuni permanetis, nihil accipientes; propterea quod rogo vos accipere cibum pro salute vestra quia nullius vestrum capillus de capite peribit."

Et cum haec dixisset, sumens panem gratias egit Deo in conspectu omnium; et cum fregisset coepit manducare. Animaequiores autem facti omnes, et ipsi sumpserunt cibum. Eramus vero universae animae in navi ducentae septuaginta sex. Et satiati cibo alleviabant navem, iactantes triticum in mare.

Cum autem dies factus esset, terram non agnoscebant; sinum vero quendam considerabant habentem litus, in quem cogitabant, si possent, eiicere navem. Et cum ancoras sustulissent committebant se mari, simul laxantes iuncturas gubernaculorum; et levato artemone, secundum aurae flatum tendebant ad litus.

Et cum incidissemus in locum dithalassum, impegerunt navem; et prora quidem fixa manebat immobilis, puppis vero solvebatur a vi maris. Militum autem consilium fuit ut custodias occiderent, ne quis cum enatassent effugeret. Centurio autem volens servare Paulum prohibuit fieri, iussitque eos qui possent natare emittere se primos, et evadere, et ad terram exire. Et ceteros alios in tabulis ferebant, quosdam super ea quae de navi erant. Et sic factum est, ut omnes animae evaderent ad terram.

They spend the winter on the island of Malta, receiving much kindness from the inhabitants.

Et cum evasissemus, tunc cognovimus quia Melita insula vocabatur; barbari vero praestabant non modicam humani-
90 tatem nobis. Accensa enim pyra reficiebant nos omnes, propter imbrem qui imminebat et frigus. Cum congregasset autem Paulus sarmentorum aliquantam multitudinem, et imposuisset super ignem, vipera a calore cum processisset, invasit manum eius. Ut vero viderunt barbari pendentem
95 bestiam de manu eius, ad invicem dicebant: "Utique homicida est homo hic; qui cum evaserit de mari, ultio non sinit eum vivere." Et ille quidem excutiens bestiam in ignem, nihil mali passus est. At illi existimabant eum in tumorem converten-dum, et subito casurum et mori. Diu autem illis exspectanti-
100 bus, et videntibus nihil mali in eo fieri, convertentes se dicebant eum esse deum.

In locis autem illis erant praedia principis insulae, nomine Publii; qui nos suscipiens triduo benigne exhibuit. Contigit autem patrem Publii febribus et dysenteria vexatum iacere.
105 Ad quem Paulus intravit; et cum orasset, et imposuisset ei manus, salvavit eum. Quo facto omnes qui in insula habebant infirmitates accedebant et curabantur. Qui etiam multis honoribus nos honoraverunt, et navigantibus imposuerunt quae necessaria erant.

The final stage of the journey.

110 Post menses autem tres navigavimus in navi Alexandrina quae in insula hiemaverat, cui erat insigne Castorum. Et cum venissemus Syracusam, mansimus ibi triduo. Inde circum-legentes devenimus Rhegium; et post unum diem, flante austro, secunda die venimus Puteolos. Ubi inventis fratribus,
115 rogati sumus manere apud eos dies septem; et sic venimus Romam. Et inde cum audissent fratres, occurrerunt nobis usque ad Appii Forum ac Tres Tabernas; quos cum vidisset Paulus, gratias agens Deo accepit fiduciam.

Cum autem venissemus Romam, permissum est Paulo
manere sibimet cum custodiente se milite.

NOTES

Line 1. *navigare eum:* "that he *was* to sail"; not simply an accusative
and infinitive.
3. *Ascendentes:* The present participle is common in New Testament
Latin, where it often has a past sense, as in English. The voyage
began from Caesarea.
navem Adrumetinam: "a ship of Adrumetum"—an interesting error.
Luke's Greek text tells us that the ship was from Adramyttium,
a rather insignificant town in Asia Minor not far from Troy. Jerome,
writing at a time when maps and reference books were virtually
unknown, misinterpreted the Greek as meaning "a ship of
Adrumetum"—the capital of Byzacium in the province of Africa.
4. *sustulimus:* from the verb *tollo*, "we raised"—*i.e.*, the anchor (the same
sense is found in lines 8, 29, 42). Most of the story of Paul's voyage
is written in the first person; Luke, the author, probably used an
account written by one of Paul's companions. Occasionally there are
rather abrupt changes to the third person (e.g., *legebant*, line 29).
perseverante . . . Thessalonicensi: "with Aristarchus, a Macedonian
from Thessalonica, continuing to travel with us"—ablative absolute
including a present participle (also in lines 14, 28, 40). Aristarchus
had also been with Paul at Ephesus (Acts xix, 29).
7. *ire:* The infinitive is found dependent upon a wider range of verbs than
in C.L. It is used again with *permitto* in line 120.
8. *subnavigavimus:* "we sailed in the lee of"—*i.e.*, they kept to the east
of Cyprus, which provided some shelter from the prevailing wind.
9. *propterea quod essent:* See Introductory Notes 5; but the subjunctive
here may be used to represent the thought in the minds of the sailors.
So also *possent* in line 75.
11. *navem Alexandrinam:* We learn later that this ship carried a cargo of
grain and 276 passengers and crew.
13. *multis diebus:* "for many days". For use of the ablative see I.N. 1(*a*).
19. *ieiunium:* the fast of the Day of Atonement. This was at the beginning
of October; the sailing season was nearly over. Paul was an experi-
enced traveller who had already been shipwrecked on three occasions.
However, it was only natural that the centurion followed the advice
of the professional sailors.
20. *video quoniam . . . :* For the use of this construction in place of an
accusative and infinitive see I.N. 2(*a*).
24. *aptus . . . ad hiemandum:* "suitable for passing the winter".
25. *si . . . possent:* The subjunctive expresses an idea of purpose: "in the
hope that they might winter".

27. *ad africum et ad corum :* "facing the south-west and north-east winds". There is today a harbour called Phenika in this part of Crete, but it is odd that the sailors should choose a harbour which was exposed to the prevailing winds.

29. *legebant :* "they coasted along".

30. *euroaquilo :* "north-easter", which would blow them away from the sheltering south coast of Crete.

31. *conari in ventum :* "make any headway against the wind".

32. *data nave :* We must supply *vento*. The ship was given to the wind— *i.e.*, it was allowed to run before the wind.

34. *scapham :* The ship's boat, previously towed behind, is now with difficulty secured on board in order to prevent it from being broken up in the heavy seas.

 adiutoriis . . . accingentes : "undergirding" or "frapping". In the days of wooden ships heavy ropes were sometimes wrapped under the keel and right over the ship in order to prevent the timbers working loose from the ribs of the ship. *adiutoriis* would refer to the tackle and pulleys which would be necessary to control the heavy ropes.

35. *Syrtim :* The Syrtes were sandbanks off the North African coast, for which they were heading.

 summisso vase : "after lowering some equipment". The meaning is uncertain; perhaps a sea-anchor was fashioned and lowered over the side in order to reduce the rate of drift towards the Syrtes.

36. *Valida :* This adjective receives additional emphasis from its position at the beginning of the sentence, separated from *tempestate*.

37. *iactum fecerunt :* "they lightened ship". It would then ride higher in the waves. On the next day they jettison more equipment.

42. *Oportebat . . . non tollere :* literally "It behoved not to set sail"—*i.e.*, "You ought not to have set sail." *Oportet* is used again in lines 47 and 50 to express this idea of duty or destiny.

43. *iniuriam . . . et iacturam :* *iniuria* refers to damage to the ship, *iactura* to loss of the cargo.

44. *esse :* For this use of the infinitive see I.N. 4.

45. *praeterquam navis :* *navis* is genitive and *amissio* supplied from the previous phrase: "except for the loss of the ship".

47. *donavit . . . omnes :* "has granted the lives of all".

48. *estote :* imperative of *esse*; "be of good courage".

49. *credo . . . quia :* For this construction see I.N. 2(*a*).

52. *Adria :* Adriatic Sea; clearly the name was applied more widely then.

53. *summittentes bolidem :* "swinging the lead"—*i.e.*, taking soundings.

58. *sub obtentu quasi :* "under the pretence that".

60. *manserint :* In English we are less accurate in our use of tenses; "unless these men stay".

62. *sumere :* For this use of the infinitive see I.N. 4.

63. *Quartadecima die hodie . . .* We should say "Today is the fourteenth day that . . ."

 exspectantes : "in suspense".

71. *triticum:* not their provisions, but the cargo of corn. When this was jettisoned the ship would draw less water, and so would get nearer to the shore before running aground.

74. *sinum:* often identified as St Paul's Bay, in the north-east of Malta.

75. *si possent:* See note to line 9 above.

76. *committebant se mari:* literally "they entrusted themselves to the sea". This cannot here mean that they threw themselves overboard, but rather that they now entrusted their ship to the mercy of the sea as they ran it aground.
   laxantes iuncturas gubernaculorum: "loosening the lashings of the steering oars". The *gubernacula* are the two long oars at the stern, used for steering; they have been fastened up out of the water while the ship has been riding at anchor.

77. *levato artemone:* The artemon was the small foresail. When this is raised, the ship has steerage-way without being driven ashore fast.

79. *in locum dithalassum:* a place where there were cross-currents.

82. *ne quis:* "so that no-one".

84. *qui possent:* The subjunctive is used because Luke is reporting indirectly the instructions of the centurion.

85. *quosdam:* Supply *ferebant* from the previous clause.

88. *cognovimus quia:* For this construction see I.N. 2(*a*).

91. *congregasset:* a shortened form of *congregavisset.*

96. *cum evaserit:* *cum* has the force of "although".

97. *nihil mali:* partitive genitive equivalent to "no harm".

98. *eum in tumorem convertendum:* literally "they thought that he must turn into a swelling"—*i.e.,* "they thought that he would swell up".

102. *principis:* the "headman" of the island.

104. *iacere:* "to be sick".

108. *navigantibus:* Supply *nobis:* "they provided what was necessary for us when we set sail".

110. *Post menses . . . tres:* They stayed in Malta for the winter months— November to February.

111. *insigne Castorum:* "the sign of Castor and Pollux". The ship probably had a figurehead of these two gods—particularly suitable as they were the protecting gods of sailors.

112. *triduo:* ablative for extent of time. See I.N. 1(*a*).

114. *fratribus:* fellow-Christians.

115. *manere:* For this use of the infinitive see I.N. 4. We read that Paul spent two years in Rome under open arrest. We do not know whether he was ever brought to trial; perhaps his accusers failed to appear. Tradition says that he suffered martyrdom in Rome, perhaps in the time of Nero's persecution of A.D. 64.

120. *sibimet:* Paul is to keep himself *to* himself. We should simply say "to lodge by himself".

Text

Actus Apostolorum (Biblia Sacra, Marietti, 1959), xxvii, 7 – xxviii, 16.

2. In Defence of Christianity

For the first century of its existence the Christian Church drew almost all its converts from the lower classes—slaves, labourers, artisans. It made little impact on the educated pagan world; the handful of Roman writers who refer to Christianity regard it as just another popular superstition. But by the end of the second century it was penetrating all classes of society and was provoking an opposition which grew more violent every day.

Previously there had been sporadic attacks by violent mobs, and the Roman authorities had sometimes taken steps against the Christians in deference to local outbursts of popular dislike; but now it began to gain converts from the educated classes, and this gave rise to literary attacks from men of culture and learning. These in turn provoked reasoned defences of the new faith such as the *Octavius* of Minucius Felix (about A.D. 200). In this extract he not only defends the conduct of Christians, but also attacks the traditional gods of Rome and the popular mystery religions.

Minucius Felix illustrates the foolish contradictions found in the mystery religions and the Olympian Gods.

Considera denique sacra ipsa et ipsa mysteria: invenies exitus tristes, fata et funera et luctus atque planctus miserorum deorum. Isis perditum filium cum Cynocephalo suo et calvis sacerdotibus luget, plangit, inquirit, et Isiaci miseri caedunt

pectora et dolorem infelicissimae matris imitantur; mox invento   5
parvulo gaudet Isis, exsultant sacerdotes, Cynocephalus inventor gloriatur, nec desinunt annis omnibus vel perdere quod
inveniunt vel invenire quod perdunt. Nonne ridiculum est vel
lugere quod colas vel colere quod lugeas? Haec tamen,
Aegyptia quondam, nunc et sacra Romana sunt.   10

Quid? Formae ipsae et habitus nonne arguunt ludibria et
dedecora deorum vestrorum? Vulcanus claudus deus et
debilis, Apollo tot aetatibus levis, Aesculapius bene barbatus,
etsi semper adulescentis Apollinis filius, Neptunus glaucis
oculis, Minerva caesiis, bubulis Iuno, pedibus Mercurius   15
alatis, Pan ungulatis, Saturnus compeditis. Ianus vero frontes
duas gestat, quasi et aversus incedat; Diana interim est alte
succincta venatrix, et Ephesia mammis multis et uberibus
exstructa, et Trivia trinis capitibus et multis manibus horrifica.

He argues that invisibility is no proof that the Christian
God does not exist. God is present in the whole of the world
that he created.

At enim quem colimus deum, nec ostendimus nec videmus.   20
Immo ex hoc deum credimus, quod eum sentire possumus,
videre non possumus. In operibus enim eius et in mundi
omnibus motibus virtutem eius semper praesentem aspicimus,
cum tonat, fulgurat, fulminat, cum serenat. Nec mireris, si
deum non vides: vento et flatibus omnia impelluntur, vibran-   25
tur, agitantur, et sub oculis tamen non venit ventus et flatus.
In sole adeo, qui videndi omnibus causa est, videre non
possumus: radiis acies summovetur, obtutus intuentis hebe-
tatur, et, si diutius inspicias, omnis visus exstinguitur. Quid?
Ipsum solis artificem, illum luminis fontem possis sustinere,   30
cum te ab eius fulgoribus avertas, a fulminibus abscondas?
Deum oculis carnalibus vis videre, cum ipsam animam tuam,
qua vivificaris et loqueris, nec aspicere possis nec tenere?

Sed enim deus actum hominis ignorat et in caelo constitutus
non potest aut omnes obire aut singulos nosse. Erras, o homo,   35

et falleris; unde enim deus longe est, cum omnia caelestia terrenaque et quae extra istam orbis provinciam sunt, deo cognita, plena sint? Ubique non tantum nobis proximus, sed infusus est. In sole adeo rursus intende: caelo adfixus, sed
40 terris omnibus sparsus est; pariter praesens ubique interest et miscetur omnibus, nusquam eius claritudo violatur. Quanto magis deus auctor omnium ac speculator omnium, a quo nullum potest esse secretum, tenebris interest, interest cogitationibus nostris quasi alteris tenebris!
45 Non tantum sub illo agimus sed et cum illo, ut prope dixerim, vivimus.

The Christian's readiness to die for his beliefs.

Quam pulchrum spectaculum deo, cum Christianus cum dolore congreditur, cum adversum minas et supplicia et tormenta componitur, cum strepitum mortis et horrorem carni-
50 ficis intrepidus inculcat, cum libertatem suam adversus reges et principes erigit, soli deo, cuius est, cedit. Vos ipsi calamitosos viros fertis ad caelum, ut Mucium Scaevolam, qui, cum errasset in regem, perisset in hostibus, nisi dextram perdidisset. Et quot ex nostris non dextram solam, sed totum corpus uri,
55 cremari sine ullis eiulatibus pertulerunt, cum dimitti praesertim haberent in sua potestate! Viros cum Mucio vel cum Aquilio aut Regulo comparo? Pueri et mulierculae nostrae cruces et tormenta, feras et omnes suppliciorum terriculas inspirata patientia doloris inludunt. Nec intellegitis, o miseri,
60 neminem esse, qui aut sine ratione velit poenam subire aut tormenta sine deo possit sustinere.

NOTES

1. *mysteria:* "mystery-religions". Many religious cults had taken root in Rome. The cult of Isis had come from Egypt, where Isis was worshipped as the great goddess who brought fertility to the fields. She was the wife of Osiris and mother of Horus and Anubis (Cynocephalus—the dog-headed god). In mid-November there was a great festival which incorporated the grief of Isis at the loss of Osiris and

28

Horus, and her joy at their rediscovery. This symbolizes the death of the old year and the birth of the new.

4. *luget, plangit, inquirit*: Minucius often puts three words together without any connecting *et*. See also lines 24 and 25.

7. *nec desinunt*: Negative expressions are common in Latin: "and they continue every year to lose what they find".

9. *colas ... lugeas*: The subjunctives show that this is a general idea—*i.e.*, "Is it not ridiculous to weep over a thing that you worship?"

10. *et*: "also".

12. *Vulcanus*: the blacksmith of the gods. Homer tells the story (*Iliad*, I, 586–594) that Jupiter in a rage once threw him out of Olympus. He landed at Lemnos and broke both his legs.

13. *tot aetatibus*: descriptive ablative—*i.e.*, "so many years old".
    Aesculapius: the god of healing, an art which he learnt from his father, Apollo, and from Chiron, the centaur.

15. *caesiis, bubulis*: *oculis* must be supplied from the previous phrase. So also, in Greek, Athene was called γλαυκῶπις ("grey-eyed") and Hera βοῶπις ("ox-eyed").

16. *ungulatis ... compeditis*: *pedibus* must be supplied from the previous phrase. Mercury, being the messenger of the gods, wore *talaria*—the winged sandals; Pan, a god of the woods and fields, was always represented as goat-footed; Saturnus was dethroned by his son, Jupiter, and imprisoned in Tartarus.

17. *incedat*: The subjunctive with *quasi* introduces an imaginary idea: "as if he walks backwards". *et*—"as well as forwards".
    Diana: the Greek Artemis, a goddess with many forms and functions. Minucius mentions three aspects introduced by the words *interim*, *Ephesia*, *Trivia*. First she is the goddess of hunting; then as the goddess worshipped in the temple at Ephesus she is an Asiatic mother-goddess; finally her statues erected at cross-roads were provided with three heads, indicating her triple function as goddess of the moon, of hunting, and of the underworld.

20. *At enim*: introduces an imaginary objection: "But, you may say, we do not depict, nor do we see the god that we worship."

21. *hoc ... quod*: "We believe him to be a god from the fact that ..."

24. *Nec mireris*: jussive subjunctive: "Do not be surprised ..."

27. *In sole*: The sense of the argument indicates that this must mean "At the sun".
    videndi: gerund; the sun, "which is the means of seeing".

28. *acies*: The basic meaning of this word is the sharp edge of a sword; here it is transferred to the keen vision of the eye.
    obtutus intuentis: "the sight of a person gazing at the sun".

29. *inspicias*: The subjunctive expresses the unlikelihood of anyone doing such a foolish thing: "if you were to look at".
    Quid?: prepares us for an indignant question: "Why, could you bear ... ?"

30. *possis*: "could you bear?"—less definite than *potes* ("can you bear?").

31. *cum:* governs both *avertas* and *abscondas.*
34. *Sed enim:* introduces a further argument from the opposition.
36. *unde:* "from what is God ever absent . . . ?"
38. *cognita:* probably refers particularly to the previous phrase—"things which are outside this universe" (and therefore known only to God, not to man).
    plena: Supply *Deo:* "filled with God".
39. *caelo adfixus:* i.e., the sun.
41. *Quanto magis . . . !*" "How much more then . . . ! "
44. *quasi alteris tenebris:* "just as in darkness of a different sort".
46. *dixerim:* "as I might almost say", potential subjunctive.
47. *Quam pulchrum spectaculum . . . :* Supply *est.* "What a glorious sight it is for God when a Christian . . .". There follow five verbs, all dependent on *cum* and all with *Christianus* as their subject.
51. *Vos ipsi:* i.e., Roman non-Christians.
52. *Mucius Scaevola:* Soon after the expulsion of the Tarquin Kings from Rome, Mucius entered the camp of Lars Porsena, the Etruscan king who was besieging Rome in an effort to restore the Tarquins. He killed a scribe in mistake for the king, but was set free by Porsena after displaying his bravery by thrusting his right hand into the fire.
54. *uri, cremari:* Supply *et.*
55. *cum dimitti:* "when, moreover, they had it in their power to be set free"—i.e., by putting a pinch of incense on the altar dedicated to the Emperor, thereby recognizing his divinity.
56. *Viros:* emphatically placed: "Is it only men that I compare . . . ?"
57. *Aquilio:* Manius Aquilius, defeated by Mithridates in 88 B.C. He fled to Pergamum. He was later surrendered and tortured to death.
    Regulo: Regulus was captured by the Carthaginians in 255 B.C. He is reputed to have been sent to Rome under oath in order to arrange peace; he then urged the Romans not to make peace, and on his return to Carthage was put to death by being kept awake until he died.
    mulierculae: The diminutive form is used to rouse additional sympathy in the reader.
60. *aut:* In English we often omit the first "or".

Text

Minucius Felix, Octavius (Edition Budé, 1964), Chapters 22, 32, and 37.

3. The Martyrdom of St Alban

Christians were suspected of indulging in arson, incest, infanticide, and cannibalism. They were also looked upon as traitors since they steadfastly refused to offer sacrifice to the Roman gods or to burn incense before the image of the Emperor—actions which adherents of other religions regarded as a mere formality, but which a Christian regarded as a denial of Christ.

Personal jealousy and mob-violence were the commonest causes of the sporadic persecution of the first two centuries, but by the third century Christianity was becoming so widespread that the Roman authorities began to regard it as a threat to their power, and so they attempted to destroy it. Two Emperors in particular (Decius in A.D. 250 and Diocletian in A.D. 303) issued specific edicts which ordered every citizen to sacrifice to the gods in the presence of a Roman official. Many Christians died for their faith on these occasions.

We read very little about persecutions in Britain. Traditionally the first British martyr was St Alban, who was executed during the final persecution in the time of Diocletian. The story is told by the Venerable Bede, a monk who had entered the monastery of St Benedict at Jarrow in A.D. 679 at the age of seven. There he was educated, and in due course became a monk, teacher, and scholar. There, in A.D. 731, he wrote the *Ecclesiastical History*—the story of Christianity in Britain.

Alban gives hospitality to a Christian, and is so impressed by him that he takes his place when soldiers come to arrest him.

Qui videlicet Albanus, paganus adhuc, cum perfidorum principum mandata adversum Christianos saevirent, clericum quendam persecutores fugientem hospitio recepit; quem dum orationibus continuis ac vigiliis die noctuque studere con-
5 spiceret, subito divina gratia respectus, exemplum fidei ac pietatis illius coepit aemulari, ac salutaribus eius exhortationibus paulatim edoctus, relictis idolatriae tenebris, Christianus integro ex corde factus est. Cumque praefatus clericus aliquot diebus apud eum hospitaretur, pervenit ad aures nefandi
10 principis confessorem Christi, cui necdum fuerat locus martyrii deputatus, penes Albanum latere. Unde statim iussit milites eum diligentius inquirere. Qui cum ad tugurium martyris pervenissent, mox se sanctus Albanus pro hospite ac magistro suo, ipsius habitu, id est caracalla, qua vestiebatur, indutus,
15 militibus exhibuit, atque ad iudicem vinctus perductus est.

The magistrate discovers the trick, questions Alban, and orders him to sacrifice to the Roman gods. Alban refuses.

Contigit autem iudicem ea hora, qua ad eum Albanus adducebatur, aris adsistere, ac daemonibus hostias offerre. Cumque vidisset Albanum, mox ira succensus nimia, quod se
20 ille ultro pro hospite, quem susceperat, militibus offerre ac discrimini dare praesumpsisset, eum iussit pertrahi: "Quia rebellem," inquiens, "ac sacrilegum celare quam militibus reddere maluisti, ut contemptor divum meritam blasphemiae suae poenam lueret, quaecumque illi debebantur supplicia, tu
25 solvere habes, si a cultu nostrae religionis discedere temptas."
At sanctus Albanus, qui se ultro persecutoribus fidei Christianum esse prodiderat, nequaquam minas principis metuit; sed accinctus armis militiae spiritalis, palam se iussis parere nolle pronuntiabat. Tum iudex: "Cuius," inquit,

Facing page: Apollo the lizard-slayer (statue of Praxiteles
32 in the Vatican Museum) *By courtesy of Phaidon Press Ltd*

APOLLO SAVROTTONO
DI PRASSITELE

Aesculapius
By courtesy of the British Museum

"familiae vel generis es?" Albanus respondit: "Quid ad te 30
pertinet, qua sim stirpe genitus? Sed si veritatem religionis
audire desideras, Christianum iam me esse, Christianisque
officiis vacare cognosce." Ait iudex: "Nomen tuum quaero,
quod sine mora mihi insinua." At ille: "Albanus," inquit, "a
parentibus vocor, et Deum verum ac vivum, qui universa 35
creavit, adoro semper, et colo." Tum iudex repletus iracundia
dixit: "Si vis perennis vitae felicitate perfrui, diis magnis
sacrificare ne differas." Albanus respondit: "Sacrificia haec,
quae a vobis redduntur daemonibus, nec auxiliari subiectis
possunt, nec supplicantium sibi desideria vel vota complere. 40
Quin immo, quicunque his sacrificia simulacris obtulerit,
aeternas inferni poenas pro mercede recipiet."

He is condemned to death.

His auditis, iudex nimio furore commotus, caedi sanctum
Dei confessorem a tortoribus praecipit, autumans se verberibus, quam verbis non poterat, cordis eius emollire constan- 45
tiam. Qui cum tormentis adficeretur acerrimis, patienter haec
pro Domino, immo gaudenter ferebat. At ubi iudex illum
tormentis superari, vel a cultu Christianae religionis revocari
non posse persensit, capite eum plecti iussit.

A miracle so impresses the executioner that he declares
himself ready to die with Alban.

Cumque ad mortem duceretur, pervenit ad flumen, quo 50
murus ab arena, ubi feriendus erat, meatu rapidissimo divide-
batur; viditque ibi non parvam hominum multitudinem
utriusque sexus, condicionis diversae et aetatis, quae sine
dubio divinitatis instinctu ad obsequium beatissimi con-
fessoris ac martyris vocabatur, et ita fluminis ipsius occupabat 55
pontem, ut intra vesperam transire vix posset. Denique
cunctis paene egressis, iudex sine obsequio in civitate substi-
terat. Igitur sanctus Albanus, cui ardens inerat devotio mentis
ad martyrium ocius pervenire, accessit ad torrentem, et

C

60 dirigens ad caelum oculos, illico siccato alveo, vidit undam,
incluso meatu, suis cessisse ac viam dedisse vestigiis, ut omnes
agnoscerent etiam torrentem martyri obsequium detulisse.
Qui videlicet fluvius, ministerio persoluto, devotione completa,
officii testimonium relinquens, reversus est ad naturam. Quod
65 cum inter alios etiam ipse carnifex, qui eum percussurus erat,
vidisset, festinavit ei, ubi ad locum destinatum morti venerat,
occurrere, divino nimirum admonitus instinctu, proiectoque
ense, quem strictum tenuerat, pedibus eius advolvitur, multum
desiderans, ut cum martyre, vel pro martyre, quem percutere
70 iubebatur, ipse potius mereretur percuti.

Both Alban and the executioner are put to death.

Dum ergo is ex persecutore factus esset collega veritatis et
fidei, ac iacente ferro esset inter carnifices iusta cunctatio,
montem cum turbis reverentissimus Dei confessor ascendit.
In huius ergo vertice sanctus Albanus dari sibi a Deo aquam
75 rogavit, statimque ante pedes eius fons perennis exortus est.
Decollatus itaque martyr fortissimus ibidem accepit coronam
vitae, quam repromisit Deus diligentibus se. Sed ille qui piis
cervicibus impias manus intulit, gaudere super mortuum non
est permissus; namque oculi eius in terram una cum beati
80 martyris capite deciderunt. Decollatus est ibi etiam tum miles
ille, qui antea superno nutu correptus, sanctum Dei confessorem ferire recusavit.

Impressed by the miracles, the magistrate ends the persecution.

Tum iudex, tanta miraculorum caelestium novitate per-
culsus, cessari mox a persecutione praecepit, honorem referre
85 incipiens caedi sanctorum, per quam eos opinabatur prius a
Christianae fidei posse devotione cessare. Passus est autem
beatus Albanus die X Kalendarum Iuliarum iuxta civitatem
Verolamium, quae nunc a gente Anglorum Verlamacaestir
sive Vaeclingacaestir appellatur, ubi postea, redeunte tem-

porum Christianorum serenitate, ecclesia est mirandi operis 90
atque eius martyrio condigna exstructa.

1. *perfidorum principum:* *princeps* was a title often used by Roman
   Emperors. The persecutions were most severe in the eastern part of
   the Roman Empire, under Diocletian, and Galerius who succeeded
   him in A.D. 305. Notice that by the time that Bede was writing many
   words had acquired new meanings in ecclesiastical Latin. In these
   opening lines *paganus* and *perfidus* both mean heathen, *oratio* prayer,
   gratia grace, *salutaris* saving, *sanctus* saint.
5. *divina gratia respectus:* "visited by divine grace".
8. *integro ex corde:* "heart and soul".
   aliquot diebus: The ablative sometimes expresses length of time. See
   I.N. 1(*a*).
9. *pervenit:* impersonal: "it came to the ears . . . that . . . "
10. *principis:* clearly not the Emperor, but the local magistrate.
    fuerat . . . deputatus: In late Latin *fueram* often replaces *eram* in
    pluperfect passive. See I.N. 7.
13. *martyris:* Alban is referred to as a martyr and as St Alban in anticipa-
    tion of what is about to happen.
19. *ira succensus nimia:* It is not clear how the magistrate knew that a
    substitution had been made.
23. *contemptor divum:* in apposition: "so that he might pay the due
    penalty for his unbelief, as a despiser of the gods".
25. *solvere habes:* *habeo* here has its colloquial sense of "have to". "You
    have to suffer whatever punishment was due to him".
28. *accinctus . . . spiritalis:* "equipped with the armour for spiritual
    warfare". Bede must have had in mind the famous verses from Eph.
    vi, 11–17.
31. *sim . . . genitus:* subjunctive of indirect question: "Why does it
    concern you of what family I am?"
33. *vacare:* "to devote oneself to".
34. *quod:* This is not really a subordinate idea: "I am asking your name;
    tell it to me without delay."
37. *perennis vitae:* not in the Christian sense of the phrase: "If you wish
    to enjoy the pleasure of living any longer in this world . . . "
38. *ne differas:* = *noli differre.*
41. *Quin immo:* introduces an even stronger objection: "Why, on the
    contrary . . ."
    obtulerit: In English we are not so exact in our use of tenses: "Whoever
    offers . . ."
45. *quam:* refers to the following *constantiam*, which is placed for em-
    phasis at the end of the sentence. *Posse* has to be supplied with

35

emollire. There is a play of words with *verberibus* and *verbis*: "thinking that with wounds he could weaken the steadfastness of spirit that he was unable to weaken with words".

46. *cum*: "although".
48. *superari*: parallel with *revocari*; both infinitives are dependent on *non posse persensit.*
54. *divinitatis instinctu*: The same sense is expressed later by the phrase *divino ... instinctu*: "by divine inspiration" (line 67).
    obsequium: This word occurs three times in the next few lines; the first time it means "escorting"; on the second occasion it has a more concrete meaning—the magistrate was left "without his retinue of servants", on the third occasion it has the usual classical meaning of "obedience".
56. *intra vesperam*: "before evening"; when they would presumably go home.
57. *paene*: with *cunctis.*
    in civitate: *civitas* had by this time also acquired the meaning of "city".
61. *suis ... vestigiis*: The order of words suggests that *suis* is ablative, and that a further *vestigiis* must be supplied for it: "He saw that the water, its flow being checked, had receded from his feet and had afforded a passage to them."
66. *ei*: governed by *occurrere.*
71. *Dum ... esset*: *dum* here has the meaning "since".
72. *iusta cunctatio*: "a natural delay".
76. *coronam ... diligentibus se*: a quotation from the Epistle of St James, i, 12.
79. *est permissus*: This passive use of *permitto* would not have been possible in Classical Latin. For the infinitive *gaudere* see note on I, line 7.
81. *superno nutu correptus*: "influenced by the will of heaven".
84. *cessari*: an impersonal passive: "ordered an end to be made of persecution".
85. *caedi*: dative of *caedes*: "beginning to show respect for the slaughter of the saints through which ... "
87. *die X*: the tenth day before the Kalends of July—*i.e.*, June 22nd.
88. *Verlamacaestir*: The original Roman name, Verulamium, has received the Anglo-Saxon form of *castra* as a suffix. In Vaeclingacaestir the first part of the name recalls the early name for Watling Street, the road from London to Wroxeter upon which St Albans is situated.

Text

Bede, *Historia Ecclesiastica Gentis Anglorum* (O.U.P., 1956), Book I, Chapter 7.

4. The Uselessness of the Temple of Concord

The persecution under Diocletian and Galerius was the last. In A.D. 313 the Emperor Constantine issued the Edict of Milan which proclaimed toleration for Christianity. The final victory came in A.D. 394, when Theodosius closed the temples and prohibited the offering of sacrifices to pagan gods.

But barbarian tribes were threatening the very existence of the Roman Empire: the Goths and the Vandals were invading Italy, Gaul, Spain, and Africa. For a time there was chaos caused by the breakdown of the social and political system of Rome, but the invasions did not bring the complete destruction of civilization, for these invasions were really tribal migrations, and although the invaders often looted and murdered the inhabitants, they were also concerned with finding fresh homes for themselves.

In the end order emerged, and it was the continuing influence of the Church which upheld civilization and integrated the new inhabitants with the old. However, at the time of the invasions those who still opposed Christianity and upheld the worship of the old gods of Rome declared that the fall of Rome was due entirely to the abandonment of the worship of Jupiter and the other gods who had protected Rome in the previous centuries.

One of the refutations of these charges came from Augustine, Bishop of Hippo, in North Africa: between A.D. 412 and

426 he published in instalments a work entitled *De Civitate Dei*, a survey of the whole of Roman history. There he analysed the real reasons for the failure of Rome, and urged that the world might be saved by the introduction of Christian principles into government.

———

The land-reforms of the Gracchi were the cause of riots and the assassination of the proposers.

Initium autem civilium malorum fuit seditiones Gracchorum agrariis legibus excitatae. Volebant enim agros populo dividere, quos nobilitas perperam possidebat. Sed iam vetustam iniquitatem audere convellere periculosissimum, immo
5 vero, ut res ipsa docuit, perniciosissimum fuit. Quae funera facta sunt, cum prior Gracchus occisus est! Quae etiam, cum alius frater eius non longo interposito tempore! Neque enim legibus et ordine potestatum, sed turbis armorumque conflictibus nobiles ignobilesque necabantur. Post Gracchi
10 alterius interfectionem Lucius Opimius consul, qui adversus eum intra Urbem arma commoverat, eoque cum sociis oppresso et exstincto ingentem civium stragem fecerat, cum quaestionem haberet iam iudiciaria inquisitione ceteros persequens, tria milia hominum occidisse perhibetur. Percussor
15 Gracchi ipsius caput, quantum grave erat, tanto auri pondere consuli vendidit; haec enim pactio caedem praecesserat.

What a splendid idea to build a temple to the Goddess of Concord on the very spot where so many citizens met their death!

Eleganti sane senatus consulto eo ipso loco, ubi funereus tumultus ille commissus est, ubi tot cives ordinis cuiusque ceciderunt, aedes Concordiae facta est, ut Gracchorum poenae
20 testis contionantum oculos feriret memoriamque compungeret. Sed hoc quid aliud fuit quam irrisio deorum, illi deae templum construere, quae si esset in civitate, non tantis dissensionibus dilacerata corrueret? Nisi forte sceleris huius rea Concordia,

38

quae deseruerat animos civium, meruit in illa aede tamquam
in carcere includi.   25

It would have been more sensible to appease the Goddess
of Discord.

Cur enim, si rebus gestis congruere voluerunt, non ibi
potius aedem Discordiae fabricarunt? Periculose Romani tam
mala dea irata vivere voluerunt nec Troianum excidium
recoluerunt originem ab eius offensione sumpsisse. Ipsa
quippe quia inter deos non fuerat invitata, trium dearum litem   30
aurei mali suppositione commenta est; unde rixa numinum
et Venus victrix, et rapta Helena et Troia deleta. Quapropter,
si forte indignata, quod inter deos in Urbe nullum templum
habere meruit, ideo iam turbabat tantis tumultibus civitatem,
quanto atrocius potuit irritari, cum in loco illius caedis, hoc   35
est in loco sui operis, adversariae constitutam aedem videret!

The power of the Goddess of Concord is shown by the
century of civil war which followed!

Praeclarum vero seditionis obstaculum aedem Concordiae,
testem caedis suppliciique Gracchorum, contionantibus
opponendam putarunt. Quantum ex hoc profecerint, indicant
secuta peiora. Laborarunt deinceps contionatores non exem-   40
plum devitare Gracchorum, sed superare propositum, Lucius
Saturninus tribunus plebis et Gaius Servilius praetor et
multo post Marcus Drusus, quorum omnium seditionibus
caedes primo iam tunc gravissimae, deinde socialia bella
exarserunt, quibus Italia vehementer adflicta et ad vastitatem   45
mirabilem desertionemque perducta est. Bellum deinde
servile successit et bella civilia. Quae proelia commissa sunt,
quid sanguinis fusum, ut omnes fere Italae gentes, quibus
Romanum maxime praepollebat imperium, tamquam saeva
barbaries domarentur!   50

NOTES

1. *Gracchorum agrariis legibus:* During the second century B.C. the
number of landowners in Italy steadily diminished; the gulf between

rich and poor widened as large estates developed owned by comparatively few citizens. Tiberius Gracchus in 133 B.C. and his brother Gaius in 123 B.C. began a redistribution of land; the resentment which this provoked resulted in riots in Rome and the assassination of both brothers.

4. *periculosissimum :* "it was very dangerous, even disastrous as events proved . . . "

6. *Quae etiam :* Supply *funera facta sunt* from the previous exclamation.

8. *ordine potestatum : potestas* here has the concrete meaning "magistrate".

10. *Lucius Opimius consul :* 121 B.C.

11. *arma commoverat :* Opimius had been instructed by the Senate to take emergency measures against Gaius; he raised a force of citizens, and overpowered and killed many supporters of Gaius; then, after perfunctory trials, he executed a further 3000.

15. *quantum . . . tanto :* literally "he sold the head for as large a weight of gold as the head was heavy"—*i.e.,* for a weight of gold equal to the weight of the head.

17. *Eleganti :* emphatic and ironic. The force could be expressed by an exclamation: "What a splendid decision it was on the part of the Senate that a Temple of Concord should be built on the very spot!"

18. *ordinis cuiusque :* "of every class of society"; there were three classes—the senators, the knights, and the people.

20. *testis :* in apposition: "so that, as a witness to the punishment of the Gracchi, it [*i.e.,* the Temple] might strike the eyes of the assembled citizens . . . "

21. *hoc :* anticipates the infinitive *construere.* "But what was this other than a mockery of the gods—to build . . . "

23. *dilacerata :* Supply *civitas* as the subject of *corrueret :* "if this goddess were in the state, it would not have fallen rent by such discord". *Nisi forte :* ironic.

27. *Periculose :* emphatic: "It was to their peril that the Romans . . . " *tam mala dea irata :* "with so great a goddess angry with them".

29. *ab eius offensione :* as explained in the following sentence.

30. *non fuerat invitata :* Discordia was not invited to the marriage of Peleus and Thetis.
    trium dearum litem : Juno, Venus, and Minerva disputed each other's claim to the golden apple, inscribed "for the fairest", which the Goddess of Discord had thrown into the midst of the guests.

32. *Venus victrix :* Paris awarded the prize to Venus and was rewarded with her assistance in abducting Helen from Sparta.

32–6. The argument is that if the Goddess of Discord could arouse such riots as occurred at the time of the Gracchi because she had no temple then how much angrier would she be (*quanto atrocius*) when she saw a temple to Concord at the very scene of her triumph.

37. *Praeclarum :* emphatic and ironic.
    seditionis obstaculum : Latin uses the genitive, whereas we say "an obstacle to civil war".

39. *opponendam* [*esse*]: gerundive in agreement with *aedem*: "They thought that a Temple of Concord ought to be placed in the sight of the speakers as they haranged the mob" (*contionantibus*).

putarunt: = *putaverunt*. (So also *Laborarunt*, line 40.)

profecerint: perfect subjunctive in a clause introduced by the interrogative *quantum*: "The worse disasters that followed show how much they gained . . ." This is, of course, ironic.

41. *propositum*: agrees with *exemplum* supplied from the previous clause: " . . . but to surpass the example already offered".

Lucius Saturninus: Used mob-violence in support of Marius in 103 B.C. Later, Saturninus and his confederate, Servilius, fell foul of Marius and were victims of his mob. Marcus Livius Drusus gained the support of Italian agitators by promising to obtain Roman citizenship for all Italians. He was assassinated in 91 B.C.

43. *quorum omnium*: It is best in English to begin a fresh sentence: "From the riots of all these men . . ."

44. *socialia bella*: the Social War (90–88 B.C.) between Rome and her Italian allies. The Italians were demanding full Roman citizenship, and in the end Rome was forced to grant it.

46. *Bellum . . . servile*: the Slave War (73–71 B.C.) against thousands of runaway slaves who plundered Italy under the leadership of Spartacus. Crassus defeated them and crucified 6000 along the Appian Way.

47. *bella civilia*: notably the war between Caesar and the Pompeians (49–45 B.C.), the war between Antony and Octavian, on the one side, and Brutus and Cassius on the other (43–42 B.C.), and finally the war between Octavian and Antony culminating in the Battle of Actium (31 B.C.).

48. *quid sanguinis*: "how much blood was shed!"

quibus: "by means of whom" or "with whose assistance".

Text

Augustine, *De Civitate Dei* (Teubner, 1909), Book III, Chapters 24, 25, and 26.

5. St Brendan on Ailbe's Island

When the Church was no longer an object of persecution and the age of mass-conversions arrived there were many who felt that the standard of the Christian life had fallen. They saw the Church opening its doors to half-converted pagans and barbarians, and they decided to withdraw from a world where martyrdom was a thing of the past, and where it now cost nothing to be a Christian. Some of those who withdrew lived the lives of hermits in the deserts or on isolated islets; others still felt the need for the society of sincere fellow-Christians, and in this way the monastic way of life developed.

One of its centres was Ireland, a country which had remained outside the Roman world and was unaffected by Christianity until the missionary work of St Patrick in the fifth century. This work was so effective that at his death in A.D. 461 the number of monasteries and Christian communities gained for Ireland the name "Isle of Saints". But these monasteries were not places of retirement from the world, but bases for further missionary journeys. One of the most remarkable characteristics of the Celtic monks was their delight in making pilgrimages and voyages, the most famous being that of St Columba to Iona in about A.D. 563.

Another monk famous for his travels was St Brendan, born about A.D. 500 near Tralee; he became an abbot and died in County Galway, where he lies buried at Clonfort. In the course of his voyages he visited Scotland, the Orkneys, and

Shetland, but in course of time he was credited with many fictitious exploits. We do not know the author of the fictional *Navigatio Sancti Brendani* (written perhaps in the tenth century), in which St Brendan is in search of the Terra Repromissionis. In this particular episode he arrives at Ailbe's Isle, where he finds a model monastery already in existence.

St Brendan and his companions land on Ailbe's Isle.

Igitur sanctus pater cum sua familia per oceani aequora huc atque illuc agitabatur per tres menses. Nihil poterant videre nisi caelum et mare. Reficiebantur semper per biduum aut triduum.

Quadam vero die apparuit illis insula non longe, et cum 5
appropinquassent ad litus, traxit illos ventus a portu. Et ita
per quadraginta dies navigabant per insulae circuitum, nec
poterant portum invenire. Fratres vero qui in nave erant
coeperunt Dominum deprecari cum fletu ut illis adiutorium
praestaret. Vires enim eorum prae nimia lassitudine paene 10
defecerant. Cum autem permansissent in crebris orationibus
per triduum et in abstinentia, apparuit illis portus angustus,
tantum unius navis receptio, et apparuerunt illis duo fontes
ibidem, unus turbidus et alter clarus. Porro fratres festinabant
cum vasculis ad hauriendam aquam. Intuens vir Dei illos ait, 15
"Filioli, nolite peragere illicitam rem sine licentia seniorum
qui in hac insula commorantur. Tribuent namque vobis has
aquas spontanee quas modo vultis furtim bibere."

They are met by a monk and led to a monastery.

Igitur descendentibus illis de navi et considerantibus quam
partem ituri essent, occurrit eis senex nimiae gravitatis, 20
capillis niveo colore et facie clarus, qui tribus vicibus se ad
terram prostravit antequam oscularetur virum Dei. At vero
sanctus Brendanus et qui cum eo erant elevaverunt eum de
terra. Osculantibus autem se invicem, tenuit manum sancti
patris idem senex et ibat cum eo per spatium quasi unius 25

stadii ad monasterium. Tunc sanctus Brendanus cum fratribus
suis stetit ante portam monasterii et dixit seni, "Cuius est
istud monasterium aut quis praeest illi, vel unde sunt qui
commorantur hic?" Itaque sanctus pater diversis sermonibus
30 interrogabat senem et nunquam ab illo poterat unum responsum accipere, sed tantum incredibili mansuetudine manu
silentium insinuabat.

They are welcomed by the abbot.

Statim ut agnovit sanctus pater illius loci decretum, fratres
suos admonebat, dicens, "Custodite ora vestra a locutionibus,
35 ne polluantur isti fratres per vestram scurrilitatem." His
interdictis verbis, ecce undecim fratres occurrerunt obviam
cum capsis et crucibus et hymnis, dicentes istud capitulum,
"Surgite, sancti, de mansionibus vestris et proficiscimini
obviam veritati. Locum sanctificate, plebem benedicite, et nos
40 famulos vestros in pace custodire dignemini." Finito iam
versiculo praedicto, pater monasterii osculatus est sanctum
Brendanum et suos socios per ordinem. Similiter et sui famuli
osculabantur familiam sancti viri.

Data pace vicissim, duxerunt illos in monasterium, sicut
45 mos est in occidentalibus partibus ducere fratres per orationes.
Post haec abbas monasterii cum monachis coepit lavare pedes
hospitum et cantare antiphonam: "Mandatum novum".

The visitors share a meal with the monks and learn some
of the wonders of the island.

His finitis, cum magno silentio duxit illos ad refectorium et
pulsato signo surrexit unus ex fratribus patris monasterii et
50 coepit ministrare mensam panibus miri candoris et quibusdam
radicibus incredibilis saporis. Sedebant autem mixtim fratres
cum hospitibus per ordinem, et inter duos fratres semper
panis integer ponebatur. Idem minister pulsato signo minis-
trabat potum fratribus.

55 Abbas quoque hortabatur fratres, cum magna hilaritate
dicens: "Ex hoc fonte quem hodie furtim bibere voluistis, ex

eo modo facite caritatem cum iucunditate et timore Dei. Ex alio fonte turbido quem vidistis lavantur pedes fratrum omni die, quia omni tempore calidus est. Panes vero quos videtis nobis ignotum est ubi praeparantur aut quis portat ad nostrum 60 cellarium. Sed tamen notum est nobis quod ex Dei magna elemosina ministrantur servis suis per aliquam subiectam creaturam. Nos sumus hic viginti quattuor fratres. Omni die habemus duodecim panes ad nostram refectionem, inter duos singulos panes. In festivitatibus et in dominicis diebus 65 integros panes singulis fratribus addit Deus, ut cenam habeant ex fragmentis. Modo in adventu vestro duplicem annonam habemus, et ita nutrit nos Christus a tempore sancti Patricii et sancti Aelbei, patris nostri, usque modo per octoginta annos. Attamen senectus aut languor in membris nostris minime 70 amplificatur. In hac insula nihil ad comedendum indigemus quod igni paratur. Neque frigus aut aestus superat nos un- quam. Et cum tempus missarum venit aut vigiliarum, incen- duntur luminaria in nostra ecclesia, quae duximus nobiscum de terra nostra divina praedestinatione, et ardent usque ad 75 diem, et non minuitur ullum ex illis luminaribus."

They go to the monastery chapel for vespers.

Postquam biberunt tribus vicibus, abbas solito more pul- savit signum, et fratres unanimiter cum magno silentio et gravitate levaverunt se a mensa, antecedentes sanctos patres ad ecclesiam. Gradiebantur vero post illos sanctus Brendanus 80 et praedictus pater monasterii. Cum ergo intrassent in ecclesiam, ecce alii duodecim fratres exierunt obviam illis, flectentes genua cum alacritate. Sanctus vero Brendanus, cum illos vidisset, dixit: "Abba, cur isti non refecti sunt nobiscum simul?" Cui ait pater: "Propter vos, quia non potuit nostra 85 mensa omnes nos capere in unum. Modo reficientur et nihil illis deerit. Nos autem intremus in ecclesiam et cantemus vesperas, ut fratres nostri qui modo reficiuntur possint ad tempus cantare vesperas post nos."

Brendan describes the chapel.

90   Dum autem perfinissent debitum vespertinale, coepit sanctus Brendanus considerare quomodo illa ecclesia erat aedificata. Erat enim quadrata tam longitudinis quam et latitudinis, et habebat septem luminaria, tria ante altare quod erat in medio, et bina ante alia duo altaria. Erant enim altaria de
95 cristallo quadrato facta et eorum vascula similiter de cristallo, id est patinae, calices et urceoli, et cetera vasa quae pertinebant ad cultum divinum, et sedilia xxiiii per circuitum ecclesiae. Locus vero ubi abbas sedebat erat inter duos choros. Incipiebat enim ab illo una turma et in illo finiebat, et alia turma
100 similiter. Nullus ex utraque parte ausus erat praesumere inchoare versum nisi praedictus abbas. Non in monasterio vox ulla audiebatur, nec ullus strepitus. Si aliquid necesse erat alicui fratri, ibat ante abbatem et genuflectebat coram illo, postulans in corde suo quae necessitas poscebat. Statim
105 sanctus pater accepta tabula et graphio, per revelationem Dei scribebat et dabat fratri qui ab illo consilium postulabat.

    Cum autem sanctus Brendanus haec omnia inter se consideraret, dixit ei abbas: "Pater, iam tempus est ut revertamur ad refectorium, ut omnia fiant cum luce." Et ita fecerunt ad
110 hunc modum, sicut ad refectionem. Finitis omnibus secundum ordinem cursus diei, omnes cum magna alacritate festinabant ad completorium. At vero abbas cum inchoasset praedictum versiculum, id est "Deus, in adiutorium meum", et dedissent simul honorem Trinitati, incipiebant versiculum cantare,
115 dicentes: "Iniuste egimus, iniquitatem fecimus. Tu qui pius es pater, parce nobis, Domine. In pace in id ipsum dormiam et requiescam, quoniam tu, Domine, singulariter in spe constituisti me." Post haec cantabant officium quod pertinet ad hanc horam.

The abbot explains the silence of the monks and foretells the destiny of the visitors.

120   Iam consummato ordine psallendi, omnes egrediebantur

46

foras fratres ad illorum singulas cellulas, accipientes hospites secum. Abbas vero cum sancto Brendano residebat in ecclesia, exspectantes adventum luminis. Interrogavit vero sanctus Brendanus sanctum patrem de illorum silentio et conversatione, quomodo ita possent in humana carne. 125

Tunc praedictus pater cum immensa reverentia et humilitate respondit: "Abba, coram Christo meo fateor: octoginta anni sunt postquam venimus in hanc insulam. Nullam vocem humanam audivimus excepto quando cantamus Deo laudes. Inter nos viginti quattuor vox non excitatur nisi per signum 130 digiti aut oculorum, et hoc tantum a maioribus natu. Nullus ex nobis sustinuit infirmitatem carnis aut spirituum qui vagantur circa humanum genus, postquam venimus in hanc insulam."

Sanctus Brendanus ait: "Licet nobis nunc hic esse annon?" 135 Qui ait: "Non licet, quia non est Dei voluntas. Cur me interrogas, pater? Nonne revelavit tibi Deus quae te oportet facere, antequam huc venisses ad nos? Te enim oportet reverti ad locum tuum cum xiiii fratribus tuis. Ibi enim praeparavit Deus locum sepulturae vestrae. Duo vero, qui 140 supersunt, unus peregrinabitur in insula quae vocatur anchoritarum, porro alter morte turpissima condemnabitur apud inferos."

The lamps of the chapel are lit supernaturally.

Cum haec intra se talia loquerentur, ecce illis videntibus sagitta ignea dimissa per fenestram incendit omnes lampades 145 quae erant positae ante altaria. Quae confestim reversa est foras praedicta sagitta. Tamen lumen pretiosum remansit in lampadibus. Iterum interrogavit beatus Brendanus: "A quo exstinguentur mane luminaria?" Cui ait sanctus pater: "Veni et vide sacramentum rei. Ecce, tu vides candelas ardentes in 150 medio vasculorum. Tamen nihil de illis exurit, ut minus sint aut decrescant, neque remanebit ulla favilla, quia spiritale lumen est." Sanctus Brendanus ait: "Quomodo potest in

47

corporali creatura lumen incorporale corporaliter ardere?"
155 Respondit senex: "Nonne legisti rubum ardentem in monte
Sinai? Et tamen remansit ipse rubus inlaesus ab igne."

Evigilantibus totam noctem usque mane, sanctus Brendanus
petivit licentiam proficiscendi in suum iter. Cui ait senex:
"Non, pater. Tu debes nobiscum celebrare Nativitatem
160 Domini usque ad octavas Epiphaniae." Mansit igitur sanctus
pater cum sua familia praedictum tempus cum xxiiii patribus
in insula quae vocatur Ailbei.

NOTES

1. *cum sua familia*: There were sixteen monks with St Brendan.
3. *Reficiebantur*: Evidently their food-supply was strictly rationed.
6. *appropinquassent*: = *appropinquavissent*.
8. *in nave*: The boat was described in an earlier chapter; it was an Irish
   'curach', a wooden framework covered with animal hides and
   caulked. It had a mast and a sail.
13. *tantum ... receptio*: "a shelter for only one ship".
15. *ad hauriendam aquam*: gerundive to express purpose: "in order to
    draw water".
    vir Dei: i.e., St Brendan.
19. *descendentibus*: Since *eis* is repeated with *occurrit*, this initial phrase
    is probably ablative absolute: "as they disembarked ... "
20. *nimiae gravitatis*, ... *niveo colore*: Both ablative and genitive cases
    are used for description.
22. *oscularetur*: The subjunctive perhaps suggests that the prostration was a
    necessary priority, but in late Latin the subjunctive with *antequam*
    often has no sense of purpose. See I.N. 5(*a*).
26. *stadii*: A *stadium* is about 200 yards.
31. *tantum*: "only", as in line 13 above.
33. *loci decretum*: Evidently the monks of the island were under a vow
    of silence.
40. *dignemini*: subjunctive, with the same force as the previous impera-
    tives.
44. *Data pace ... per orationes ... coepit lavare*: The Rule of St Benedict
    contains the following order about hospitality: "*occurratur ei a priore
    ... pacis osculum non prius offeratur nisi oratione praemissa ...
    ducantur ad oratorium ... pedes hospitibus omnibus tam abbas quam
    cuncta congregatio lavet.*"
47. *Mandatum novum*: "A new commandment I give unto you ..."
    (St John xiii, 34) spoken by Jesus when He washed the disciples'
    feet. From *mandatum* we derive the word "Maundy".

48

St Albans Abbey from the Roman Wall
By courtesy of Photo Precision Ltd

A reconstruction of the Temple of Concord in the Roman Forum
By courtesy of Centaur Books Ltd

multitudo nonsolum palatio· uerum etiam regno
non inmerito· uideretur onerosa· Ipse tamen p̄
magnitudine animi / huiuscemodi pondere
minime grauabatur· Cum etiam ingentia in
commoda laude liberalitatis ac bone famae
mercede compensaret· Corpore fuit amplo
atq; robusto· statura eminenti quae tamen
iustam non excederet· Nam septem suorum
pedum p̄ceritate eius constat habuisse mensura·
Apice capitis rotundo· oculis p̄grandibus ac
uegetis· Naso paululum mediocritatem exce
denti· canitie pulchra· facie laeta & hilari· In
deformae auctoritas ac dignitas tam stanti quā
sedenti plurima adquirebatur· quam quia ceruix
obesa & breuior· uenterq; proiectior uideretur ;
Tamen haec caeterorum membrorum celabat
aequalitas· incessu firmo totaq; corporis habi
tudine uirili· Uoce clara quidem sed quae minus
corporis formae conueniret· Ualitudine prospera
p̄ter quod ante quā· decederet perquatuor annos
crebro febribus corripiebatur· adextremum etiā
uno pede claudicaret· & tunc quidem plura suo
arbitratu quā medicorum consilio faciebat· quos

Facsimile of part of a ninth-century manuscript of Einhard's
Life of Charlemagne now in the National Museum in Vienna.
The facsimile is of lines 36-55 of our text.
By courtesy of the Österreichische Nationalbibliothek, Wien

50. *ministrare mensam panibus :* We use the same expression, "to serve the table".
51. *mixtim . . . per ordinem :* "alternately along the line".
57. *facite caritatem :* "take your allowance"; *caritas* is the regular word in ecclesiastical Latin for a monk's allowance of food and drink.
60. *praeparantur :* For the indicative see I.N. 3.
61. *notum est . . . quod :* "it is known that"; for this form of construction see I.N. 2(*a*).
62. *elemosina :* "mercy, alms".
65. *in dominicis diebus :* "on the days of our Lord"—*i.e.* Sundays. From *dominicus* is derived the French *dimanche*.
71. *ad comedendum :* gerund; "we lack nothing for eating"—*i.e.*, for our meals.
73. *missarum : missa* the Mass.
    vigiliarum : vigilia the Vigil before a special saint's day.
88. *vesperas :* There were seven occasions during daylight when monks were expected to sing chants and offer prayers. These *Horae Canonicae* are *Matutina, Prima, Tertia, Sexta, Nona, Vespera,* and *Completorium.*
90. *Dum :* here with the meaning of *cum* (as in Section 3, line 71).
    debitum vespertinale : "their evening duty".
91. *erat aedificata :* For the indicative in an indirect question see I.N. 3.
96. *patinae, calices et urceoli :* vessels used in the celebration of Mass. *Patina* is a paten to hold the bread, *calix* is a chalice for the wine, *urceolus* is a ewer for water.
109. *ut omnia fiant cum luce :* The Rule of St Benedict stipulates "*sed et omni tempore sive cena sive refectionis hora, sic temperetur ut luce fiant omnia*".
112. *completorium :* Compline—the last service of the day.
113. *Deus, in adiutorium meum :* Psalm lxx, 1.
115. *Iniuste egimus :* Some of these words are from Psalm iv, 8.
120. *psallendi :* gerund: "now that the duty of chanting was completed".
142. *morte turpissima :* In a later chapter we read how he was caught in the lava-flow from a volcano.
150. *sacramentum rei :* "the sacred mystery".
158. *proficiscendi :* gerund: "permission to depart".
160. *ad octavas Epiphaniae :* "to the eighth day of Christmas".

Text

Navigatio Sancti Brendani (University of Notre-Dame Press, 1959), Chapter 12.

6. The Emperor Charlemagne

In Section 5 the religious life and the organization of a monastery have been described. A further aspect of the life of monasteries was their educational work, a work that was greatly developed by the Emperor Charlemagne (A.D. 742–814).

Charlemagne became King of the Franks on the death of his father in 768. Thereafter he steadily extended his rule, until, by the end of the eighth century, he was master of the whole of Continental Europe included in Western Christendom—Germany, Belgium, France, Northern Italy, and Northern Spain. His coronation by the Pope in A.D. 800 as *Imperator Romanum gubernans imperium* ("Emperor ruling the Roman Empire") gave religious and legal recognition to his vast power.

To govern this empire Charlemagne needed educated administrators. In answer to this practical need, and to satisfy his own desire to strengthen and purify the Christian faith, Charlemagne embarked on a policy of encouraging and promoting learning. This revival of learning (the Carolingian Renaissance) took the form of founding cathedral schools and monasteries, and safeguarding and copying the sacred books, the works of the Fathers, and secular Latin literature. Had it not been for Charlemagne a very large part of Latin literature (including Caesar, Sallust, Lucretius, Tacitus, and much of Cicero) would have been lost to civilization.

Another important function of the cathedral and monastery schools was the training of priests and scholars. One of the most distinguished of these was Einhard (A.D. 770–840). Einhard was born in Eastern Frankland, near the modern German town of Kassel. He went to school in the neighbouring monastery of Fulda, and from there to the palace school of Charlemagne at Aix-la-Chapelle. Here he came into contact with Alcuin, an English scholar who was, to use a modern term, cultural adviser to the Emperor. Einhard's working life was spent first in the service of Charlemagne, and, on his death, in the service of Charlemagne's son and successor, Louis the Pious. Einhard was a teacher in the palace school, writer, and, later, biographer of Charlemagne.

His *Life of Charlemagne*, from which these extracts are taken, was written between 814 and 821. Though closely modelled on the work of the Roman writer Suetonius, it yet manages to give a vivid and individual picture of the Emperor. Some modern critics object that the picture is biased, uncritical, and overkind. For example, the very considerable streak of cruelty in the Emperor is glossed over by Einhard; nor is the Emperor's harsh treatment of his daughters (see lines 30–34 below) explained. Perhaps this biography may be regarded as a semi-official life of Charlemagne, with all the advantages and disadvantages that this type of life entails.

Charlemagne and his Children

Liberos suos ita censuit instituendos ut tam filii quam filiae primo liberalibus studiis, quibus et ipse operam dabat, erudirentur. Tum filios, cum primum aetas patiebatur, more Francorum equitare, armis ac venatibus exerceri fecit, filias vero lanificio adsuescere coloque ac fuso, ne per otium torperent, 5 operam impendere atque ad omnem honestatem erudiri iussit.

Ex his omnibus duos tantum filios et unam filiam, priusquam moreretur, amisit, Karolum, qui natu maior erat, et

Pippinum, quem regem Italiae praefecerat, et Hruodtrudem, quae filiarum eius primogenita et a Constantino Graecorum imperatore desponsata erat. Quorum Pippinus unum filium suum Bernhardum, filias autem quinque, Adalhaidem, Atulam, Gundradam, Berthaidem ac Theoderadam, superstites reliquit. In quibus rex pietatis suae praecipuum documentum ostendit, cum filio defuncto nepotem patri succedere et neptes inter filias suas educari fecisset. Mortes filiorum ac filiae pro magnanimitate, qua excellebat, minus patienter tulit, pietate videlicet, qua non minus insignis erat, compulsus ad lacrimas.

Nuntiato etiam sibi Hadriani Romani pontificis obitu, quem in amicis praecipuum habebat, sic flevit ac si fratrem aut carissimum filium amisisset. Erat enim in amicitiis optime temperatus, ut eas et facile admitteret et constantissime retineret, colebatque sanctissime quoscumque hac adfinitate sibi coniunxerat.

Filiorum ac filiarum tantam in educando curam habuit ut numquam domi positus sine ipsis cenaret, numquam iter sine illis faceret. Adequitabant ei filii, filiae vero pone sequebantur, quarum agmen extremum ex satellitum numero ad hoc ordinati tuebantur. Quae cum pulcherrimae essent et ab eo plurimum diligerentur, mirum dictu quod nullam earum cuiquam aut suorum aut exterorum nuptum dare voluit, sed omnes secum usque ad obitum suum in domo sua retinuit, dicens se earum contubernio carere non posse.

His Love of Foreigners

Amabat peregrinos et in eis suscipiendis magnam habebat curam, adeo ut eorum multitudo non solum palatio verum etiam regno non immerito videretur onerosa. Ipse tamen prae magnitudine animi huiuscemodi pondere minime gravabatur, cum etiam ingentia incommoda laude liberalitatis ac bonae famae mercede compensaret.

Corpore fuit amplo atque robusto, statura eminenti, quae tamen iustam non excederet—nam septem suorum pedum proceritatem eius constat habuisse mensuram—apice capitis rotundo, oculis praegrandibus ac vegetis, naso paululum mediocritatem excedente, canitie pulchra, facie laeta et hilari. 45 Unde formae auctoritas ac dignitas tam stanti quam sedenti plurima adquirebatur. Quamquam cervix obesa et brevior venterque proiectior videretur, tamen haec ceterorum membrorum celabat aequalitas. Incessu firmo totaque corporis habitudine virili. Voce clara quidem, sed quae minus corporis 50 formae conveniret. Valetudine prospera, praeter quod, antequam decederet, per quattuor annos crebro febribus corripiebatur, ad extremum etiam uno pede claudicaret. Et tunc quidem plura suo arbitratu quam medicorum consilio faciebat, quos paene exosos habebat quod ei in cibis assa, quibus 55 adsuetus erat, dimittere et elixis adsuescere suadebant.

Exercebatur assidue equitando ac venando; quod illi gentilicium erat quia vix ulla in terris natio invenitur quae in hac arte Francis possit aequari. Delectabatur etiam vaporibus aquarum naturaliter calentium, frequenti natatu corpus 60 exercens; cuius adeo peritus fuit ut nullus ei iuste valeat anteferri. Ob hoc etiam Aquisgrani regiam exstruxit ibique extremis vitae annis usque ad obitum perpetim habitavit. Et non solum filios ad balneum, verum optimates et amicos, aliquando etiam satellitum et custodum corporis turbam 65 invitavit, ita ut nonnumquam centum vel eo amplius homines una lavarentur.

Habits, Daily Life

In cibo et potu temperans, sed in potu temperantior quippe qui ebrietatem in qualicumque homine, nedum in se ac suis, plurimum abominabatur. Cibo enim non adeo abstinere 70 poterat, ut saepe quereretur noxia corpori suo esse ieiunia. Convivabatur rarissime et hoc praecipuis tantum festivitatibus,

53

tunc tamen cum magno hominum numero. Cena cotidiana
quaternis tantum ferculis praebebatur praeter assam, quam
75   venatores veribus inferre solebant, qua ille libentius quam
ullo alio cibo vescebatur. Inter cenandum aut aliquod
acroama aut lectorem audiebat. Legebantur ei historiae et
antiquorum res gestae. Delectabatur et libris sancti Augustini,
praecipueque his qui De Civitate Dei praetitulati sunt. Vini
80   et omnis potus adeo parcus in bibendo erat ut super cenam
raro plus quam ter biberet. Aestate post cibum meridianum
pomorum aliquid sumens ac semel bibens, depositis vestibus
et calciamentis, velut noctu solitus erat, duabus aut tribus
horis quiescebat. Noctibus sic dormiebat ut somnum quater
85   aut quinquies non solum expergiscendo sed etiam desurgendo
interrumperet. Cum calciaretur et amiciretur, non tantum
amicos admittebat verum etiam, si comes palatii litem aliquam
esse diceret quae sine eius iussu definiri non posset, statim
litigantes introducere iussit et, velut pro tribunali sederet, lite
90   cognita sententiam dixit; nec hoc tantum eo tempore sed
etiam quicquid ea die cuiuslibet officii agendum aut cuiquam
ministrorum iniungendum erat expediebat.

His Studies

Erat eloquentia copiosus et exuberans poteratque quicquid
vellet apertissime exprimere. Nec patrio tantum sermone
95   contentus, etiam peregrinis linguis ediscendis operam im-
pendit. In quibus Latinam ita didicit ut aeque illa ac patria
lingua orare sit solitus, Graecam vero melius intellegere quam
pronuntiare poterat. Adeo quidem facundus erat ut etiam
dicaculus appareret.
100   Artes liberales studiosissime coluit, earumque doctores
plurimum veneratus magnis adficiebat honoribus. In discenda
grammatica Petrum Pisanum diaconem senem audivit, in
ceteris disciplinis Albinum cognomento Alcuinum, item diaconem, de Britannia Saxonici generis hominem, virum
105   undecumque doctissimum, praeceptorem habuit, apud quem

54

et rhetoricae et dialecticae, praecipue tamen astronomiae ediscendae plurimum et temporis et laboris impertivit. Discebat artem computandi et intentione sagaci siderum cursum curiosissime rimabatur. Temptabat et scribere tabulasque et codicillos ad hoc in lecto sub cervicalibus 110 circumferre solebat ut, cum vacuum tempus esset, manum litteris effigiendis adsuesceret, sed parum successit labor praeposterus ac sero inchoatus.

Devotion to the Church

Religionem Christianam, qua ab infantia fuerat imbutus, sanctissime et cum summa pietate coluit; ac propter hoc 115 plurimae pulchritudinis basilicam Aquisgrani exstruxit auroque et argento et luminaribus atque ex aere solido cancellis et ianuis adornavit. Ad cuius structuram cum columnas et marmora aliunde habere non posset, Roma atque Ravenna devehenda curavit. Ecclesiam et mane et vespere, 120 item nocturnis horis et sacrificii tempore, quoad eum valetudo permiserat, impigre frequentabat; curabatque magnopere ut omnia quae in ea gerebantur cum quam maxima fierent honestate, aedituos creberrime commonens ne quid indecens aut sordidum aut inferri aut in ea remanere permitterent. 125 Sacrorum vasorum ex auro et argento vestimentorumque sacerdotalium tantam in ea copiam procuravit ut in sacrificiis celebrandis ne ianitoribus quidem, qui ultimi ecclesiastici ordinis sunt, privato habitu ministrare necesse fuisset. Legendi atque psallendi disciplinam diligentissime emendavit. 130 Erat enim utriusque admodum eruditus, quamquam ipse nec publice legeret nec nisi submissim et in commune cantaret.

Death

Extremo vitae tempore, cum iam et morbo et senectute premeretur, evocatum ad se Hludowicum filium, Aquitaniae regem, congregatis sollemniter de toto regno Francorum 135 primoribus, cunctorum consilio consortem sibi totius regni et

55

imperialis nominis heredem constituit, impositoque capiti eius
diademate Imperatorem et Augustum iussit appellari. Suscep-
tum est hoc eius consilium ab omnibus qui aderant magno
140 cum favore; nam divinitus ei propter regni utilitatem vide-
batur inspiratum. Auxitque maiestatem eius hoc factum et
exteris nationibus non minimum terroris incussit. Dimisso
deinde in Aquitaniam filio, ipse more solito quamvis senectute
confectus, non longe a regia Aquensi venatum proficiscitur,
145 exactoque in huiuscemodi negotio quod reliquum erat
autumni, circa Kalendas Novembris Aquasgrani revertitur.

Cumque ibi hiemaret, mense Ianuario febre valida correptus
decubuit. Qui statim, ut in febribus solebat, cibi sibi absti-
nentiam indixit, arbitratus hac continentia morbum posse
150 depelli vel certe mitigari. Sed accedente ad febrem lateris
dolore, quem Graeci pleurisin dicunt, illoque adhuc inediam
retinente neque corpus aliter quam rarissimo potu sustentante,
septimo postquam decubuit die, sacra communione percepta,
decessit, anno aetatis suae septuagesimo secundo et ex quo
155 regnare coeperat quadragesimo septimo, V Kal. Februarii,
hora diei tertia.

NOTES

1. *instituendos*: Supply *esse*. The gerundive implies necessity: "He
   thought his children ought to be brought up . . ."
   tam . . . quam . . .: "his daughters equally with his sons . . ."
2. *primo*: "in their early years".
4. *fecit*: "he caused" or "made".
6. *ad omnem honestatem*: "in every honourable art".
7. *Ex his omnibus*: Charlemagne had eight legitimate children.
   priusquam moreretur: An indicative would be found in C.L. There
   seems to be no special meaning attached to the subjunctive. See
   I.N. 5(*a*).
16. *fecisset*: "had caused him".
17. *pro magnanimitate . . . minus patienter tulit*: "he bore less patiently
    than the greatness of his mind . . . warranted." *Pro* = in proportion
    to.
20. *Hadriani*: Pope Hadrian died in 795.
23. *admitteret . . . retineret*: subjunctives expressing result.
24. *quoscumque*: Supply *eos* (. . . *quoscumque*).
27. *domi positus*: simply "at home".

56

29. *ex satellitum numero ad hoc ordinati:* "members of the corps of attendants stationed specially for this purpose".
31. *dictu:* supine: "it is surprising to relate that . . ."
    quod: normal M.L. See I.N. 2.
32. *nuptum:* supine expressing purpose. Translate "in marriage".
37. *prae = pro* in C.L.: "in accordance with".
41. *Corpore . . . amplo,* etc.: descriptive ablative: "of".
42. Simplified order: *constat proceritatem eius habuisse mensuram . . . septem suorum pedum.*
46. Take *stanti* and *sedenti* in agreement with *ei* understood. Literally, "From which (*unde*) very great dignity and impressiveness of presence (*formae*) were gained (for him) as much standing as sitting."
48. *videretur:* subjunctive with *quamquam.* See I.N. 5(*a*).
49. *aequalitas:* "excellent proportion". *Haec* is the object of *celabat.*
    Incessu firmo: Understand *erat.*
50. *Voce clara:* Understand *erat.*
    quae . . . conveniret: The subjunctive suggests the idea "a sort of voice which . . ."
51. *Valetudine prospera:* Understand *erat.*
52. *decederet:* subjunctive with *antequam.* No special meaning. I.N. 5(*a*).
53. *ad extremum:* Supply *vitae.*
    claudicaret: subjunctive with *praeter quod.* See I.N. 5(*a*).
56. *dimittere . . . adsuescere suadebant:* For the infinitive with *suadeo* see I.N. 4.
57. *Exercebatur:* not passive but so-called middle voice: "he used to exercise himself".
59. *possit:* subjunctive implying possibility: "could".
61. *cuius:* "in which"—swimming.
62. *Aquisgrani:* Aquaegrani, modern Aachen (or Aix-la-Chapelle, to give it its French name) was the capital of Charlemagne's Empire. It means "the waters (or springs) of Granus", referring to the medicinal springs sacred to Apollo Granus, around which the town grew.
68. *quippe qui . . . abominabatur:* A subjunctive is usually found with *quippe qui* in C.L.
71. *ut . . . quereretur:* subjunctive expressing cause: "since he would complain . . ."
78. *sancti Augustini:* St Augustine, the great Christian theologian (A.D. 354–430). An extract from the *De Civitate Dei* is given in Section 4.
83. *duabus aut tribus horis:* ablative expressing duration of time. The accusative case would be used in C.L. See I.N. 1(*a*).
87. *comes palatii:* The Count of the Palace was Charlemagne's chief minister.
    si comes . . . diceret: The subjunctive seems to express two ideas: (1) "if he should say"—possibility; (2) "whenever he said"—frequent occurrence.
88. *quae . . . non posset:* subjunctive in a relative clause in reported speech.

57

eius: Charlemagne's.

89. *velut . . . sederet :* = *velut si sederet.*

91. *quicquid . . . cuiuslibet officii :* "whatever (of) business"—partitive genitive.

agendum . . . iniungendum : gerundives expressing necessity: "whatever task he had to do or entrust to any of his ministers".

94. *vellet . . .* subjunctive expressing possibility—"whatever he might wish . . ."

96. *patria lingua :* German; now known as Old High German.

101. *veneratus :* perfect participle with the meaning of a present participle.

103. *cognomento Alcuinum :* literally "Alcuin by surname". Translate "whose surname was Alcuin". Alcuin, born in York *c.* 735, was head of the school at Charlemagne's Court till 790. Died at Tours in 804.

106. *dialecticae :* dialectic = philosophy.

107. *plurimum et temporis et laboris :* "very much [of] time and effort" —partitive genitive.

111. *circumferre :* i.e., on his travels.

112. *effigiendis :* "forming". Though deeply interested in learning, Charlemagne probably could not write.

114. *fuerat imbutus :* M.L. is fond of these extra compound tenses. See I.N. 7.

120. *devehenda curavit :* "had them transported".

121. *eum . . . permiserat : permitto* in C.L. patterns with the dative case. See I.N. 1(*b*).

124. *ne . . . permitterent :* subjunctive in the reported command after *commonens.*

125. *inferri . . . remanere :* In C.L. *ut* with subjunctive is normally found after *permitto.* See I.N. 4.

131. *quamquam legeret . . . cantaret :* See I.N. 5(*a*).

141. *inspiratum :* agrees with *consilium* from the previous part of the sentence.

142. *minimum terroris :* literally "not the least of fear"—partitive genitive. Translate: "considerable fear".

144. *venatum :* supine expressing purpose: "to hunt".

145. *exacto :* does not agree with *negotio,* but forms an ablative absolute with *quod reliquum erat autumni :* "having spent the rest of autumn in this pursuit . . ."

150. *accedente . . . retinente . . . sustentante :* ablative absolutes expressing cause.

155. *V Kal. Februarii hora diei tertia :* January 28th at 9 A.M.

Text

Einhard's Life of Charlemagne (ed. H. W. Garrod and R. B. Mowat; Oxford, 1915), Chapters 19, 21, 22, 24–26, and 30.

58

7. The Journey of Friar William de Rubruquis to the East in the Year of Grace 1253

William de Rubruquis was born *c.* 1215 in the village of Rubrouck, in French Flanders. He became a friar in the Franciscan Order and served at the Court of Louis IX (St Louis) of France, who sent him on a mission to the Emperor of the Mongols, Khan Mangu.

There had been persistent rumours that the Mongols had turned to Christianity and wished for an alliance with Western Christendom. William set out, in the spring of 1253, on an immense and hazardous journey to try to find out the true position.

Starting from Constantinople, he sailed into the Black Sea and landed on the Crimean Coast. He struck east, crossing the Don, Volga, and Ural rivers. Then, travelling south-east, he finally arrived at the camp of Khan Mangu, afterwards proceeding to his Court at Karakorum, in Mongolia, some 500 miles south of Lake Baikal—in all a journey of 5000 miles.

He found that the rumours of the Mongols' desire for friendship with Western Christendom were quite untrue. On the contrary, the haughty Mangu stressed the might of the Mongol Empire and warned the West against any interference. William sadly returned home in 1255.

The following extracts are from the journal that William wrote describing his journey. This journal was of considerable

Tartar dwellings

From *The Book of Ser Marco Polo*, translated and edited by Colonel Sir Henry Yule (John Murray, 1921)

importance in adding to the knowledge in the Western world of the geography and customs of the Eastern lands traversed by William.

Dedication

Excellentissimo Domino et Christianissimo, Lodovico Dei gratia Regi Francorum illustri, frater Willielmus de Rubruquis in ordine fratrum Minorum minimus salutem et semper triumphare in Christo. Scriptum est in Ecclesiastico de sapiente, In terram alienarum gentium transibit, bona et mala 5 in omnibus temptabit. Hoc opus, Domine mi Rex, feci: sed utinam ut sapiens et non stultus. Multi enim faciunt quod facit sapiens, sed non sapienter sed magis stulte: de quorum numero timeo me esse. Tamen quocumque modo fecerim, quia dixistis mihi quando recessi a vobis ut omnia scriberem 10 vobis quaecumque viderem inter Tartaros, et etiam monuistis ut non timerem vobis scribere longas litteras, facio quod iniunxistis; cum timore tamen et verecundia quia verba congrua mihi non suppetunt quae debeam tantae scribere Maiestati. 15

Of the Tartars and their Homes and Pasturelands

Nusquam habent manentem civitatem, sed futuram ignorant. Inter se diviserunt Scythiam, quae durat a Danubio usque ad ortum solis. Et quilibet capitaneus, secundum quod habet plures vel pauciores homines sub se, scit terminos pascuorum suorum et ubi debet pascere hieme et aestate, vere et autumno. 20 In hieme enim descendunt ad calidiores regiones versus meridiem. In aestate ascendunt ad frigidiores versus aquilonem. Loca pascuosa sine aquis pascunt in hieme quando est ibi nix, quia nivem habent pro aqua.

Portable Houses

Domum in qua dormiunt fundant super rotam de virgis 25 cancellatis cuius tigna sunt de virgis, et conveniunt in unam

parvulam rotam superius de qua ascendit collum sursum tamquam fumigatorium, quam cooperiunt filtro albo; et frequentius imbuunt etiam filtrum calce vel terra alba et
30 pulvere ossium ut albens splendeat; et aliquando nigro. Et filtrum illud circa collum superius decorant pulchra varietate picturae. Ante ostium similiter suspendunt filtrum opere polimitario variatum. Consumunt enim filtrum coloratum in faciendo vites et arbores, aves et bestias. Et faciunt tales
35 domos ita magnas quod habent triginta pedes in latitudine. Ego enim mensuravi semel latitudinem inter vestigia rotarum unius bigae viginti pedum; et quando domus erat super bigam excedebat extra rotas in utroque latere quinque pedibus ad minus. Ego numeravi in una biga viginti duos boves trahentes
40 unam domum; undecim in uno ordine secundum latitudinem bigae et alios undecim ante illos; axis bigae erat magnus ad modum arboris navis. Et unus homo stabat in ostio domus super bigam minans boves.

Portable Chests for Personal and Household Goods

Insuper faciunt quadrangulos de virgulis fissis attenuatis ad
45 quantitatem unius arcae magnae; et postea de una extremitate ad aliam elevant testudinem de similibus virgis et ostiolum faciunt in anteriore extremitate. Et postea cooperiunt illam cistam sive domunculam filtro nigro, quod similiter decorant opere polimitario vel plumario. Et in talibus arcis ponunt
50 totam supellectilem suam et thesaurum; quas ligant fortiter super bigas alteras quas trahunt cameli, ut possint transvadare flumina. Tales arcas numquam deponunt de bigis.

Disposition of Houses and Carts

Quando deponunt domus suas mansionarias, semper ver-
tunt portam ad meridiem; et consequenter collocant bigas
55 cum arcis hinc et inde prope domum ad dimidium iactum lapidis; ita quod domus stat inter duos ordines bigarum quasi inter duos muros.

Womenfolk

Matronae faciunt sibi pulcherrimas bigas, quas nescirem vobis describere nisi per picturam. Unus dives Moal sive Tartar habet bene tales bigas cum arcis ducentas vel centum. Baatu habet sedecim uxores: quaelibet habet unam magnam domum, exceptis aliis parvis, quas collocant post magnam, quae sunt quasi camerae; in quibus habitant puellae. Ad quamlibet istarum domorum appendent ducentae bigae. Et quando deponunt domus, prima uxor deponit suam curiam in capite occidentali, et postea aliae secundum ordinem suum; ita quod ultima uxor erit in capite orientali; et erit spatium inter curiam unius dominae et alterius iactus unius lapidis. Unde curia unius divitis Moal apparebit quasi una magna villa: tunc paucissimi viri erunt in ea. Una muliercula ducet viginti bigas vel triginta. Terra enim plana est. Et ligant bigas cum bobus vel camelis unam post aliam et sedebit muliercula in anteriore minans bovem, et omnes aliae pari gressu sequentur. Si contingat venire ad aliquem malum passum, solvunt eas et transducunt sigillatim; vadunt enim lento gressu, sicut agnus vel bos potest ambulare.

Sleeping Arrangements

Postquam deposuerint domus versa porta ad meridiem, collocant lectum domini ad partem aquilonarem. Locus mulierum est semper ad latus orientale, hoc est ad sinistrum domini domus cum sedet in lecto suo versa facie ad meridiem; locus vero virorum ad latus occidentale, hoc est ad dextrum. Viri ingredientes domum nullo modo suspenderent pharetram ad partem mulierum. Et super caput domini est semper una imago quasi puppa et statuuncula de filtro quam vocant fratrem domini: alia similis super caput dominae quam vocant fratrem dominae, affixa parieti; et superius inter utramque illarum est una parvula, macilenta, quae est quasi custos totius domus. Domina domus ponit ad latus suum dextrum

ad pedes lecti in eminenti loco pelliculam haedinam impletam
90 lana vel alia materia et iuxta illam statuunculam parvulam
respicientem famulas et mulieres. Iuxta ostium ad partem
mulieris est iterum alia imago cum ubere vaccino, pro
mulieribus quae mungunt vaccas. De officio feminarum est
mungere vaccas. Ad aliud latus ostii versus viros est alia statua
95 cum ubere equae pro viris qui mungunt equas.

Ceremonies Connected with Drinking

Et cum convenerint ad potandum, primo spargunt de potu
illi imagini quae est super caput domini; postea aliis imaginibus per ordinem; postea exit minister cum cipho et potu et
spargit ter ad meridiem, qualibet vice flectendo genu; et hoc
100 ad reverentiam ignis; postea ad orientem ad reverentiam
aeris: postea ad occidentem ad reverentiam aquae: ad aquilonem proiciunt pro mortuis. Quando tenet dominus ciphum
in manu et debet bibere, tunc primo antequam bibat, infundit
terrae partem suam. Si bibit sedens super equum infundit
105 antequam bibat super collum vel crinem equi. Postquam vero
minister sic sparserit ad quattuor latera mundi, revertitur in
domum et sunt parati duo famuli cum duobus ciphis ut
deferant potum domino et uxori sedenti iuxta eum sursum
in lecto. Et cum habet plures uxores, illa cum qua dormit in
110 nocte sedet iuxta eum in die; et oportet quod omnes aliae
veniant ad domum illam illa die ad bibendum; et ibi tenetur
curia illa die; et xenia quae deferuntur, illa deponuntur in
thesauris illius dominae. Bancus ibi est cum utre lactis vel
cum alio potu et cum ciphis.

Tartars' Method of Provoking Others to Drink

115 Cum dominus incipit bibere tunc unus ministrorum
exclamat alta voce: HA, et citharista percutit citharam. Et
quando faciunt festum magnum, tunc omnes plaudunt manibus et saltant ad vocem citharae, viri coram domino et
mulieres coram domina. Et postquam dominus biberit, tunc

64

exclamat minister sicut prius et tacet citharista; tunc bibunt   120
omnes in circuitu viri et mulieres; et aliquando bibunt valde
turpiter et gulose. Et quando volunt aliquem provocare ad
potum, arripiunt eum per aures et trahunt fortiter ut dilatent
ei gulam, et plaudunt et saltant coram eo. Item cum aliqui
volunt facere magnum festum et gaudium, unus accipit ciphum   125
plenum et alii duo sunt ei a dextris et a sinistris: et sic illi
tres veniunt cantantes usque ad illum cui debent porrigere
ciphum, et cantant et saltant coram eo; et cum porrigit
manum ad recipiendum ciphum, ipsi subito resiliunt et
iterum sicut prius revertuntur, et sic illudunt ei ter vel quater   130
retrahendo ciphum donec fuerit bene exhilaratus et bonum
habeat appetitum et tunc dant ei ciphum et cantant et
plaudunt manibus et terunt pedibus donec biberit.

Temples, Idols, and Religious Worship

Later in his journey William encounters many tribes who
worship false gods. He tries to draw the Priests into conversa-
tion.

Omnes sacerdotes eorum rasum habent totum caput et
barbam; sunt vestiti de croceo et servant castitatem, ex quo   135
radunt caput. Et vivunt pariter centum vel ducenti in una
congregatione. Diebus quibus intrant templum, ponunt duo
scamna et sedent e regione chorus contra chorum, habentes
libros in manibus, quos aliquando deponunt super illa
scamna; et habent capita discooperta quamdiu insunt in   140
templo, legentes in silentio et tenentes silentium. Unde cum
ingressus fuissem apud oratorium quoddam eorum et in-
venissem eos ita sedentes, multis modis temptavi eos provocare ad verba et nullo modo potui.

Dress and Equipment of the Priests

Habent etiam quocumque vadunt quemdam restem centum   145
vel ducentorum nucleorum, sicut nos portamus pater noster.
Et dicunt semper haec verba: Ou mam Hactaui, hoc est;

E   65

Deus tu nosti, secundum quod quidam eorum interpretatus est mihi. Et toties exspectant remunerationem a Deo quoties
150 hoc dicendo memoratur Dei. Circa templum suum faciunt pulchrum atrium quod bene includunt muro; et ad meridiem faciunt portam magnam in qua sedent ad colloquendum. Et super illam portam erigunt perticam longam quae emineat super totam villam. Et per illam perticam potest cognosci
155 quod domus illa sit templum Idolorum. Ista communia sunt omnibus idolatris. Quando ergo ingressus fui praedictam idolatriam inveni sacerdotes sedentes sub porta exteriore. Illi quos vidi videbantur mihi fratres Franci esse rasis barbis. Tiaras habebant in capitibus cartaceas. Istorum Iugurum
160 sacerdotes habent talem habitum quocumque vadunt; semper sunt in tunicis croceis satis strictis accincti desuper recte sicut Franci; et habent pallium super humerum sinistrum descendens involutum per pectus et dorsum ad latus dextrum.

Their Writing

Ipsi incipiunt scribere sursum et ducunt lineam deorsum,
165 et eodem modo ipsi legunt et multiplicant lineas a sinistra ad dextram. Isti multum utuntur cartis et characteribus pro sortilegio. Unde templa sua plena sunt brevibus suspensis. Et Mangu-cham mittit vobis litteras in idiomate Moal et litteratura eorum.

Their Practices and Beliefs

170 Isti comburunt mortuos suos secundum antiquum modum et recondunt pulverem in summitate pyramidis. Cum ergo sedissem iuxta praedictos sacerdotes, postquam ingressus fueram templum, et vidissem idola eorum multa magna et parva, quaesivi ab eis quid ipsi crederent de Deo. Qui
175 responderunt, "Non credimus nisi unum Deum." Et ego quaesivi, "Creditis quod ipse sit spiritus vel aliquid corporale?" Dixerunt "Credimus quod sit spiritus." Et ego, "Creditis quod numquam sumpserit humanam naturam?"

Dixerunt, "Minime." Tunc ego, "Ex quo creditis, quod non sit nisi unus spiritus, quare facitis ei imagines corporales et tot insuper? Et ex quo non creditis quod factus sit homo, quare facitis ei magis imagines hominum quam alterius animalis?" Tunc responderunt, "Nos non figuramus istas imagines Deo. Sed quando aliquis dives moritur ex nostris, vel filius vel uxor vel aliquis carus eius facit fieri imaginem defuncti et ponit eam hic; et nos veneramur eam ad memoriam eius." Quibus ego, "Tunc ergo non facitis ista nisi propter adulationem hominum." Immo dixerunt ad memoriam. Tunc quaesiverunt a me quasi deridendo: "Ubi est Deus?" Quibus ego, "Ubi est anima vestra?" Dixerunt, "In corpore nostro." Quibus ego, "Nonne est ubique in corpore tuo et totum regit, et tamen non videtur? Ita Deus ubique est et omnia gubernat, invisibilis tamen quia intellectus et sapientia est." 190

Tunc cum vellem plura ratiocinari cum illis, interpres meus fatigatus, non valens verba exprimere, fecit me tacere. 195

Their Treatment of Idols

Istorum sectae sunt Moal sive Tartari; quantum ad hoc, quod ipsi non credunt nisi unum Deum, tamen faciunt de filtro imagines defunctorum suorum et induunt eas quinque pannis pretiosissimis, et ponunt in una biga vel duabus et illas bigas nullus audet tangere. Et sunt sub custodia divinatorum 200 suorum qui sunt eorum sacerdotes. Isti divinatores semper sunt ante curiam ipsius Mangu et aliorum divitum; pauperes enim non habent eos. Et cum debent bigare, ipsi praecedunt sicut columna nubis filios Israel, et ipsi considerant locum metandi castra et post eos tota curia. Et tunc cum sit dies 205 festus sive kalendae, ipsi extrahunt praedictas imagines et ponunt eas ordinate per circuitum in domo sua. Tunc veniunt Moal et ingrediuntur domum illam et inclinant se imaginibus illis et venerantur illas. Et illam domum nemini ingredi extraneo licet. Quadam enim vice volui ingredi et multum 210 dure increpatus fui.

67

3. *in ordine fratrum Minorum:* the Franciscan Order, founded by St Francis of Assisi in 1209.
  salutem: Understand *dat.*
4. *triumphare:* Understand some such words as *te vult.*
  in Ecclesiastico: The reference is to Ecclesiasticus xxxix, 4.
6. *in omnibus:* Supply *rebus:* "in all situations".
9. *fecerim:* The subjunctive sometimes in M.L. expresses the idea of indefiniteness.
10. *dixistis . . . vobis:* William uses the plural (the Royal plural) in addressing his sovereign.
11. *viderem:* subjunctive in a subordinate clause inside a reported command.
14. *quae debeam:* The subjunctive is used to describe the type of things he ought to write: "such things as I ought . . ."
16. *futuram:* the life to come after death.
18. *secundum quod:* "according to whether . . ."
21. *In hieme:* C.L. omits the preposition.
26. *cuius:* Refers back to *domum.*
29. *terra alba:* gypsum, the mineral from which plaster of Paris is made.
30. *et aliquando nigro:* Supply *collum cooperiunt filtro.*
32. *picturae:* "of painting".
35. *ita . . . quod habent:* The C.L. would have been *tantas . . . ut* with the subjunctive.
38. *excedebat:* The subject is *domus.*
  quinque pedibus: The ablative shows by how much the house jutted out beyond the wheels.
40. *secundum latitudinem bigae:* "across the front of the cart" or "widthways to the cart".
42. *ad modum arboris navis:* literally "to the way, or fashion, of a ship's mast". Translate: "like a ship's mast".
56. *ita quod . . . stat:* "in such a way that . . . " C.L. would have *ita . . . ut* with the subjunctive.
58. *quas nescirem:* subjunctive expressing negative possibility: "which I could not . . ."
59. *Moal sive Tartar: Moal* = Mongol. Rubruquis uses *Tartari* vaguely for Tartars or Mongols. The Tartars were a wholly nomadic people living in what is now the steppe land of the U.S.S.R.; the Mongols were a more settled people inhabiting what is now Mongolia.
60. *bene:* This seems to go with *habet:* "certainly has . . . "
61. *Baatu:* the Khan Mangu's viceroy or district governor.
65. *curiam:* literally "court". Here it means "household".
66. *in capite occidentali:* "on the western extremity".
67. *ita quod . . . erit:* as line 56 above.
74. *Si contingat venire:* "Should it chance that they come". Subjunctive expressing possibility.

77. *Postquam deposuerint :* subjunctive where C.L. would have indicative. No particular meaning. See I.N. 5(*a*).

81. *locus vero :* Supply *est*.

82. *suspenderent :* subjunctive expressing the idea of usual, customary action: "would not hang . . ." This sentence stresses the fact that the men's and women's places were quite separate.

93. *De officio :* "It is the duty . . . " Literally "It is from, or part of, the duty . . . "

96. *cum convenerint :* subjunctive with *cum* meaning "when" in a sentence in which the main verb is present tense. C.L. would have the indicative. See I.N. 5(*b*).

97. *illi imagini :* literally "they sprinkle to (= on) that figure".

99. *qualibet vice :* "each time".
    flectendo : gerundive with the idea of the present participle. See I.N. 6.
    hoc : Supply *faciunt*.

102. *proiciunt :* Supply *vinum*.

103. *antequam bibat :* Often the subjunctive is used without any particular meaning in M.L. with *antequam* (see I.N. 5(*a*)), but here there seems to be some idea of purpose: "before drinking . . . "

105. *Postquam . . . sparserit :* For the subjunctive with *postquam* see I.N. 5(*a*).

110. *oportet quod omnes . . . veniant :* C.L. would have *oportet omnes venire*.

119. *postquam . . . biberit :* subjunctive with *postquam*; See I.N. 5(*a*).

126. *alii duo sunt ei a dextris :* Take *ei dextris* together = "on his right". *a dextris* = C.L. *a dextra*.

131–3. *donec fuerit . . . exhilaratus, donec habeat, donec biberit :* The subjunctives express the idea of purpose.

134–63. William is here describing the rites of Buddhism as practised by the Lamas.

135. *vestiti de croceo :* "dressed in saffron coloured garments".
    ex quo : "and because of this . . . "

141. *Unde :* "concerning these . . . " Translate: "In this connection . . . "; a M. L. meaning of *unde*.
    cum ingressus fuissem : M.L. equivalent of C.L. *ingressus essem*. See I.N. 7.

146. *pater noster :* used as an indeclinable noun: "a rosary" or string of beads used to assist the memory in the recitation of prayers.

148. *nosti :* shortened form of *novisti*.
    secundum quod : literally "according to what . . . "

149. *toties . . . quoties :* literally "how often (*quoties*) they recall God . . . so often (*toties*) do they expect . . . "

150. *memoratur :* impersonal passive—literally "it is recalled to mind".
    Dei : genitive with verbs of remembering.

153. *quae emineat :* subjunctive expressing purpose.

154. *cognosci quod :* C.L. would have accusative and infinitive construction. See I.N. 2 (*b*).

156. *ingressus fui :* For the compound see I.N. 7.

158. *fratres Franci*: French monks.
    rasis barbis: ablative absolute expressing cause: "since their beards..."
159. *Iugurum*: a sub-group of Tartars.
164. *deorsum*: They write in lines perpendicular to the page, as do the Chinese.
167. *brevibus suspensis*: "documents that are hung up". The Lamas still hang up in their temples pieces of paper or cotton bearing magical formulae or prayers.
168. *Mangu-cham*: Khan Mangu, Emperor of the Mongols.
172. *ingressis fueram*: For the compound tense see I.N. 7.
176. *Creditis quod ... sit*: For *quod* with subjunctive instead of C.L. accusative and infinitive see I.N. 2(*b*).
184. *quando*: used often in M.L. as the equivalent of C.L. *ubi*.
185. *facit fieri*: "has made".
189. *deridendo*: ablative of gerund where C.L. would have a present participle. See I.N. 6.
195. *verba*: i.e., *mea verba*.
196. *quantum ad hoc*: Supply *refert*: "as far as this [argument] is concerned, namely that (*quod*) ..."
197. *non credunt nisi unum Deum*: "believe only in one God".
204. *sicut columna nubis filios Israel*: = *sicut columna nubis praecessit filios Israel*. The reference is to Exodus xiii, 21.
205. *et post eos tota curia*: Supply *considerat locum metandi castra*.
    cum sit: C.L. would have indicative. I.N. 5(*b*).
211. *increpatus fui*: for C.L. *increpatus sum*. See I.N. 7.

Text

*Itinerarium fratris Willielmi de Rubruquis de ordine fratrum Minorum Galli,
anno gratiae 1253 ad partes Orientales* (from Hakluyt's edition of 1598,
ed. for the Hakluyt Society by C. R. Beazley, 1903).

8. Thomas More's "Utopia"

Thomas More was born in 1478. After studying at Oxford and the Inns of Court he became a lawyer, and later entered public service, where, after a brilliant career, he was appointed Lord Chancellor by Henry VIII. His period of office was, however, to end disastrously. Henry wished to divorce his wife Catharine of Aragon and to marry Anne Boleyn. Since the Pope opposed divorce Henry was obliged to break with the Pope and establish himself as the supreme head of the Church in England. More was unable to support his sovereign in what he considered to be the usurpation of the rightful authority of the Pope. He resigned the Chancellorship, declined to attend the coronation of Anne Boleyn, and refused to take the oath of supremacy acknowledging the King as the head of the Church in England. He was imprisoned in the Tower, tried and convicted, and executed in 1535.

More was at the centre of the New Learning in England, a learning that was based on the twin foundations of the literature of Greece and Rome and a purified Christianity. More studied Greek at Oxford under Grocyn, and was a skilled Latin scholar and a competent theologian. He was a close friend of Erasmus, the greatest scholar of the age, and it was at More's house that Erasmus's *In Praise of Folly* (to which Section 9 is devoted) was completed. More, however, was no isolated academic. He was deeply immersed in the

71

life and culture of his times, saw their faults and weaknesses, and wanted to help remedy them. It was in this spirit that *Utopia* was written.

This word was coined by More from the two Greek words meaning "not" and "place"—*i.e.*, nowhere. The idea was as old as Plato's *Republic*—to construct an imaginary, ideal world embodying the principles and practices noticeably lacking in the author's world. In this way a powerful criticism of the social, political, economic, and religious evils of the author's own times could be developed. In the brief extracts given below, enlightened town-planning with gardens for all is envisaged; the prime importance of agriculture for a healthy society is recognized; a way of life is outlined in which adequate leisure is at everyone's disposal and the State provides opportunities for education and cultural activities; elements of communism are introduced in the provision of free food for all; and, finally, gold, silver, and jewels are held up to ridicule.

Houses and Gardens

Plateae cum ad vecturam tum adversus ventos descriptae commode; aedificia neutiquam sordida, quorum longa et totum per vicum perpetua series conspicitur. Has vicorum frontes via pedes viginti lata distinguit. Hortus adiacet latus,
5 vicorum tergis undique circumsaeptus. Nulla domus est quae non ut ostium in plateam ita posticum in hortum habeat. Quin bifores quoque facili tractu manus apertiles ac dein sua sponte coeuntes. Quemvis intromittunt quia nihil usquam privati est. Nam domos ipsas uno quoque decennio sorte
10 commutant.

Hos hortos magnificiunt, in his vineas, fructus, herbas, flores habent; tanto nitore cultuque ut nihil fructuosius usquam viderim, nihil elegantius. Qua in re studium eorum non ipsa voluntas modo sed vicorum quoque invicem de suo
15 cuiusque horti cultu certamen accendit.

Agriculture—a Compulsory Task for All

Ars una est omnibus viris mulieribusque promiscua, agricultura, cuius nemo est expers. Hac a pueritia erudiuntur omnes, partim in schola, traditis praeceptis, partim in agros viciniores urbi quasi per ludum edocti, non intuentes modo sed per exercitandi corporis occasionem tractantes etiam. 20

One Mode of Dress for All

Nam vestes, quarum nisi quod habitu sexus discernitur et caelibatus a coniugio, una per totam insulam forma est; eademque per omne aevum perpetua; nec ad oculum indecora et ad corporis motum habilis, tum ad frigora aestusque rationem apposita. Eas, inquam, quaeque sibi familia conficit. 25

How the Utopians apportion their Day

Syphograntorum praecipuum ac prope unicum negotium est curare ac prospicere ne quisquam desideat otiosus sed uti suae quisque arti sedulo incumbat; nec ab summo mane tamen ad multam usque noctem perpetuo labore, velut iumenta, fatigatus. Nam ea plus quam servilis aerumna est, 30 quae tamen ubique fere opificum vita est, exceptis Utopiensibus qui cum in horas xxiv diem noctemque dividant, sex duntaxat operi deputant, tres ante meridiem, tres deinde rursus labori datas cena claudunt. Sub octavam horam cubitum eunt, horas octo somnus vindicat. Quicquid inter operis 35 horas ac somni cibique medium esset, id suo cuiusque arbitrio permittitur; non quo per luxum aut segnitiam abutatur sed quod ex animi sententia in aliud studii bene collocet. Sollemne est enim publicas cotidie lectiones haberi antelucanis horis. Ex omni ordine, mares simul ac feminae, 40 multitudo maxima, ad audiendas lectiones alii alias prout cuiusque fert natura, confluit. Hoc ipsum tempus tamen si quis arti suae mavult insumere, haud prohibetur. Super cenam tum unam horam ludendo producunt, aestate in hortis, hieme

45 in aulis illis communibus, in quibus comedunt. Ibi aut
musicam exercent aut se sermone recreant.

Free Food and Communal Eating

Ad has aulas prandii cenaeque, statis horis tota Sypho-
grantia convenit, aeneae tubae clangore commonefacta, nisi
qui aut in hospitiis aut domi decumbunt. Quamquam nemo
50 prohibetur, postquam aulis est satisfactum, e foro domum
cibum petere, sciunt neminem id temere facere cum neque
honestum habeatur et stultum sit deterioris parandi prandii
sumere laborem cum lautum praesto apud aulam sit.

Gold and Silver are scorned

Aurum argentumque sic Utopienses apud se habent ut ab
55 nullo pluris aestimentur quam rerum ipsarum natura meretur.
Qua quis non videt quam longe infra ferrum sunt? Ut sine
quo non hercle magis quam absque igni atque aqua vivere
mortales non queant. Cum in fictilibus e terra vitroque
elegantissimis sed vilibus tamen edant bibantque, ex auro
60 atque argento non in communibus aulis modo sed in privatis
etiam domibus matellas passim ac sordidissima quaeque vasa
conficiunt. Ad hoc catenas et compedes, quibus coercent
servos, iisdem ex metallis operantur. Postremo quoscumque
aliquod crimen infames facit, ab horum auribus anuli depen-
65 dent aurei, digitos aurum cingit, aurea torques ambit collum,
et caput denique auro vincitur. Ita omnibus curant modis ut
apud se aurum argentumque in ignominia sint.

Itaque haec tam diversa ab reliquis gentibus instituta, quam
diversas itidem animorum affectiones pariant, numquam
70 aeque mihi atque in Anemoliorum legatis inclaruit. Venerunt
hi Amaurotum dum ego aderam. Ingressi sunt legati tres cum
comitibus centum, omnes vestitu versicolori, plerique serico;
legati ipsi amictu aureo, magnis torquibus, anulis aureis in
manibus, omnibus rebus ornati quae apud Utopinienses aut
75 servorum supplicia aut infamium dedecora aut puerorum

74

nugamenta fuere. Quin pueros vidisses compellare matrem ac latus fodere: "En, mater, quam magnus nebulo margaritis adhuc et gemmulis utitur ac si esset puerulus!" At parens, "Tace," inquit, "fili; est, opinor, quispiam e morionibus legatorum."

NOTES

1. *descriptae:* Understand *sunt.*
2. *aedificia:* Understand *sunt.*
6. *ut ... ita ... :* "which does not have a front door to the road as well as a rear door to the garden".
7. *bifores ... apertiles:* Understand *sunt.*
8. *nihil ... privati:* "nothing is private". Literally "there is nothing of private"—partitive genitive.
13–15. *voluntas* and *certamen* are the subjects of *accendit; studium* is the object. *Certamen* goes closely with *vicorum.*
17. *Hac:* Understand *arte.*
18. *in agros viciniores:* Understand some such expression as "by going into ... "
19. *quasi per ludum:* "as if in play".
20. *tractantes:* "carrying out the operations".
21. *Nam vestes:* "Now, as to their clothes, of which ... " An ungrammatical sentence. *Vestes* is left high and dry without a verb. From the point of view of meaning, *vestes* is picked up by *eas* in the next sentence (line 25).
    nisi quod: "except for the fact that ... "
26. *Syphograntorum:* The Syphogrants are the elected representatives of the people. Every thirty families elect one Syphogrant to the national assembly.
28. *ab summo mane: mane* is treated as an indeclinable noun: "morning", *summus* here means "earliest".
32. *cum ... dividant:* "although they split up ... "
34. *octavam:* by our reckoning, not the ancient Roman.
36. *esset:* subjunctive expressing possibility: "might be".
37. *non quo ... abutatur sed quod ... collocet:* The subjunctive expresses purpose: "not to abuse it ... but to spend it ... "
41. *ad audiendas lectiones:* gerundive expressing purpose.
50. *postquam aulis est satisfactum:* "after the needs of the halls have been satisfied". Literally "after it has been satisfied to the halls"—impersonal passive.
55. *pluris:* "at a higher value".
56. *Qua:* "In which"—*i.e.*, their natural qualities.

quam longe . . . sunt : indicative where C.L. would have subjunctive in a
    reported question. See I.N. 3.
    Ut : "Since".
58. *in fictilibus e terra vitroque :* "in vessels made from earth and glass".
62. *Ad hoc :* "Moreover".
68. *quam diversas . . . affectiones pariant :* subjunctive in the indirect
    question introduced by *inclaruit :* "What varied attitudes of mind
    (*affectiones*) such customs (*instituta*) . . . produce, has never before
    been more clearly shown (*inclaruit*) to my mind (*mihi*) than in the
    case (*in*) of the Anemolian ambassadors."
71. *Amaurotum :* capital of Utopia.
72. *vestitu versicolori*; *amictu aureo*, etc.: ablatives of description: "in
    many-coloured raiment", etc.
76. *vidisses :* The subjunctive expresses the idea of possibility: "you
    could have seen . . . "

Text

Utopia (ed. E. Surtz and J. H. Hexter; Yale University Press, 1965),
Book II.

9. In Praise of Folly

Erasmus was born at Rotterdam in 1467, became a chorister at Utrecht Cathedral, went through the normal Classical education of those times, and proved a brilliant scholar. By the age of thirteen he is reputed to have been able to recite the whole of Terence and Horace by heart! His parents died when he was young, and his guardians, in order to provide some security for the boy, were anxious that he should enter a monastery. Somewhat against his will he eventually consented and became a Franciscan monk. The life of the monastery, however, was not to his taste, and, while remaining a Franciscan, he managed to spend the rest of his life outside monastery walls. After a period of study in Paris he lived for varying periods in England, Flanders, Italy, and Switzerland, writing, teaching, and lecturing. In England he became the friend of outstanding scholars—Thomas More, Colet, Dean of St Paul's, Linacre, and Latimer. His output of writing was enormous and included letters, essays, tracts, satires, translations, and an edition of the New Testament. While he was interested in all aspects of contemporary society, he was particularly concerned with education and learning and with religion, in both of which spheres he felt there was great need of reform.

The education and learning of his time were strait-jacketed by tradition. They clung to outworn and largely meaningless

Classical ideas. They concentrated on dry-as-dust details of grammar, syntax, and style. Erasmus represented the New Learning, a learning that was untrammelled by tradition, that was based on the individual's search for truth, that was critical, and that was concerned with the real world and real problems. This learning would be expressed in a clear Latin modelled on the great masters of Classical Latin, and would be based on Greek as well as on Latin literature.

Like More, Erasmus was deeply interested in promoting the study of Greek. Not only did Greek allow scholars to approach the New Testament afresh; it opened up a whole new civilization based upon man's curiosity and eagerness to question and challenge accepted truths and traditions. This exactly suited the restless mood of Erasmus and his friends.

This restlessness is nowhere better seen than in Erasmus's attitude to the Church. The religious life of Erasmus's day had become set in its ways. The trappings, the forms of worship, had assumed more importance than the message of the Scriptures. The morals of many priests and Church officials had become lax. Vice and corruption in the Church could no longer be ignored. In Germany Luther was starting a movement of radical reform that was to lead to the Reformation. Erasmus was not prepared to go so far and break altogether with the Church of Rome. But he used all his powers to expose and criticize existing weaknesses and to propose changes that would purify the Church.

In Praise of Folly (Moriae Encomium)

In this satirical work, from which the following extracts are taken, Erasmus, while ranging over the whole scene of human stupidity, greed, and evil, concentrates his attack in the two fields of education and learning, and the Church. The words of the book are spoken by Folly herself, who shows how she blinds mortals and leads them into living silly and wicked

lives. Man emerges as a rather pathetic figure who cannot live
without Folly.

Superstitious Practices in the Church

Folly inveighs against priests who make money out of
miracles, prodigies, and the sale of indulgences.

Ceterum illud hominum genus haud dubie totum est
nostrae farinae qui miraculis ac prodigiosis gaudent mendaciis, vel audiendis vel narrandis, nec ulla satietas talium
fabularum, cum portentosa quaedam, de spectris, de lemuri-
bus, de larvis, de inferis, de id genus milibus miraculorum   5
commemorantur; quae quo longius absunt a vero, hoc et
creduntur libentius, et iucundiore pruritu titillant aures.
Atque haec quidem non modo ad levandum horarum taedium
mire conducunt, verum etiam ad quaestum pertinent, praecipue sacrificis et contionatoribus. His rursum adfines sunt ii   10
qui sibi stultam quidem, sed tamen iucundam persuasionem
induerunt, futurum ut, si ligneum aut pictum aliquem
Polyphemum Christophorum aspexerint, eo die non sint
perituri; aut qui sculptam Barbaram praescriptis verbis
salutarit, sit incolumis e proelio rediturus; aut si quis Erasmum   15
certis diebus, certis cereolis, certisque preculis convenerit,
brevi sit dives evasurus. Iam vero Georgium etiam Herculem
invenerunt. Huius equum phaleris ac bullis religiosissime
adornatum tantum non adorant ac subinde novo quopiam
munusculo demerentur.   20
Nam quid dicam de iis qui sibi fictis scelerum condona-
tionibus suavissime blandiuntur ac purgatorii spatia veluti
clepsydris metiuntur, saecula, annos, menses, dies, horas
tamquam e tabula mathematica citra ullum errorem dime-
tientes. Aut de iis qui magicis quibusdam notulis ac preculis,   25
quasi pius aliquis impostor vel animi causa vel ad quaestum
excogitavit, freti nihil sibi non pollicentur, opes, honores,
voluptates, saturitates, valetudinem perpetuo prosperam,

vitam longaevam, senectam viridem, denique proximum
30 Christo apud superos consessum. Hic mihi puta negotiator
aliquis aut miles aut iudex, abiecto ex tot rapinis unico
nummo, universam vitae Lernam semel expurgatam putat,
totque periuria, tot libidines, tot ebrietates, tot rixas, tot
caedes, tot imposturas, tot perfidias, tot proditiones existimar
35 velut ex pacto redimi, et ita redimi ut iam liceat ad novum
scelerum orbem de integro reverti. Quid autem stultius iis,
immo quid felicius, qui septem illis sacrorum psalmorum
versiculis cotidie recitatis, plus quam summam felicitatem
sibi promittunt? Et haec tam stulta ut meipsum propemodum
40 pudeat, tamen adprobantur, idque non a vulgo modo verum
etiam a religionis professoribus.

Saints

Folly censures the idea of "local" saints and criticizes the
attribution of specific powers to particular saints.

Quid iam, nonne eodem fere pertinet cum singulae regiones
suum aliquem peculiarem vindicant divum, cumque in singulos singula quaedam partiuntur, singulis suos quosdam cul-
45 turae ritus attribuunt, ut hic in dentium cruciatu succurrat,
ille parturientibus dexter adsit, alius rem furto sublatam
restituat, hic in naufragio prosper affulgeat, ille gregem
tueatur; atque item de ceteris. Nam omnia percensere
longissimum fuerit. Sunt qui singuli pluribus in rebus
50 valeant, praecipue Deipara virgo, cui vulgus hominum plus
prope tribuit quam filio.

Schoolmasters

Schoolmasters are held up to ridicule by Folly. They are
brutal, wholly concerned with trivial details, and smug into
the bargain.

Sed ipsa stultissima sim si pergam popularium stultitiarum
et insaniarum formas enumerare. Ad eos accingar qui sapien-

The type of schoolmaster Erasmus had in mind—a contemporary picture by Holbein

tiae speciem inter mortales tenent, inter quos grammatici primas tenent, genus hominum profecto quo nihil calamatosius, nihil afflictius, nihil aeque diis invisum foret, nisi ego miserrimae professionis incommoda dulci quodam insaniae genere mitigarem. Sescentis diris obnoxii sunt ut qui semper famelici sordidique in ludis illis suis, in ludis dixi, immo in pistrinis potius ac carnificinis, inter puerorum greges consenescant laboribus, obsurdescant clamoribus, fetore paedoreque contabescant; tamen meo beneficio fit ut sibi primi mortalium esse videantur. Adeo sibi placent dum pavidam turbam minaci vultu voceque territant; dum ferulis, virgis,

65 lorisque conscindunt miseros, dumque modis omnibus suo
arbitratu saeviunt. Interim sordes illae merae munditiae
videntur, paedor amaricinum olet, miserrima illa servitus
regnum esse putatur.

Iam adde et hoc voluptatis genus quoties istorum aliquis
70 voculam vulgo incognitam in putri quapiam charta deprehenderit, puta bubsequam, bovinatorem aut manticulatorem; aut
si quis vetusti saxi fragmentum, mutilis notatum litteris,
alicubi effoderit. O Iuppiter, quae tum exultatio, qui triumphi,
quae encomia, perinde quasi vel Africam devicerint vel
75 Babylonas ceperint. Quid autem cum frigidissimos et insul-
sissimos versiculos suos passim ostentant neque desunt qui
mirentur, iam plane Maronis animam in suum pectus demi-
grasse credunt. At nihil omnium suavius quam cum ipsi inter
sese mutua talione laudant ac mirantur. Quod si quis alius
80 verbulo lapsus sit, idque forte hic oculatior deprehenderit,
quae protinus tragoediae, quae digladiationes, quae invec-
tivae?

An example is given of a grammarian who spent more than
twenty years in the pursuit of useless grammatical knowledge.

Novi quendam sexagenarium qui, ceteris rebus omissis,
annis plus viginti se torquet ac discruciat in grammatica,
85 prorsus felicem se fore ratus si tamdiu liceat vivere donec
certo statuat quomodo distinguendae sint octo partes ora-
tionis, quod hactenus nemo Graecorum aut Latinorum ad
plenum praestare valuit. Perinde quasi res sit bello quoque
vindicanda si quis coniunctionem faciat dictionem ad adverbi-
90 orum ius pertinentem. Et cum totidem sint grammaticae quot
grammatici, immo plures, quandoquidem Aldus meus unus
plus quinquies grammaticam dedit, hic nullam quantumvis
barbare aut moleste scriptam praetermittit quam non evolvat
excutiatque, nemini non invidens si quid quantumlibet inepte
95 moliatur in hoc genere, misere timens ne quis forte gloriam
hanc praeripiat et pereant tot annorum labores. Utrum

insaniam hanc vocare mavultis an stultitiam? Nam mea
quidem haud magni refert, modo fateamini meo beneficio fieri
ut animal omnium alioqui longe miserrimum eo felicitatis
evehatur ut sortem suam neque cum Persarum regibus cupiat   100
permutare.

NOTES

2. *nostrae farinae: farina*, literally "flour", here signifies "material".
   Literally: "of our material". Translate: "within my scope".
3. *vel audiendis vel narrandis:* go with *mendaciis*. Translate: "in listening
   to or describing lies".
   nec ulla satietas: Understand *est illis.*
5. *id genus:* used adverbially: "of this type".
6. *quo longius ... hoc et ... libentius:* literally, "by which the further ...
   by this even the more willingly ... " Translate: "The further away
   they are ... the more willingly ... "
11. *sibi ... induerunt:* literally, "have put on themselves" (*sibi*). Translate
    "have assumed".
12. *futurum:* future infinitive of *sum* (understand *esse*).
    futurum ut: with *persuasionem*. Literally: "the belief that it will be that
    ... " Translate: "the belief that ... "
13. *Polyphemum Christophorum:* St Christopher, who lived in Lydia, in
    Asia Minor, was executed for his Christian beliefs during the perse-
    cutions of Christians that took place under the Emperor Decius
    (A.D. 201–251). Polyphemus was the huge one-eyed giant who was
    blinded by Ulysses. In giving Christopher the epithet Polyphemus
    Erasmus is stressing the size of the statue. Translate: "Some huge
    statue of St Christopher".
14. *sculptam Barbaram:* a statue of St Barbara, martyred about the year
    A.D. 235. St Barbara was the patron saint in thunderstorms and the
    protectress of artillerymen and miners.
15. *Erasmum:* Erasmus was a bishop in Syria during the reign of the
    Emperor Diocletian (A.D. 245–313). He was appealed to in certain
    illnesses and by sailors. From him and from another saint, Desiderius,
    Erasmus took his names.
17. *Georgium ... Herculem:* St George was put to death on the orders of
    the Emperor Diocletian in A.D. 303 in Palestine. Because he was
    famous for slaying the dragon, Erasmus gives him the epithet Her-
    cules, the mythical hero credited with killing the huge water
    serpent known as the Lernaean Hydra. Translate: "They have even
    discovered their own Hercules in St George." See note below on
    line 32.
19. *tantum non adorant:* "they almost worship".
21. *sibi ... blandiuntur:* "delude themselves".

26. *animi causa :* "for the sake of entertainment".
27. *freti :* goes with the ablatives *magicis quibusdam notulis ac preculis* (line 25). *nihil . . . non :* "everything".
30. *Hic : = hoc modo :* "In this way".
   mihi, so-called ethic dative, simply means "now".
   puta : imperative of *puto*; became an invariable expression meaning "for example".
32. *Lernam :* a forest and marsh near Argos, in Greece, where the Hydra lived. (See note above to line 17.) Here *Lerna* = "cesspool".
37. *septem illis sacrorum psalmorum versiculis . . . recitatis :* verses from the Book of Psalms that the Devil is said to have indicated to St Bernard as being particularly effective.
42. *Quid iam :* "Further".
   eodem . . . pertinet : "point in the same direction"—*i.e.,* towards folly.
44. *singula quaedam :* "particular powers".
   culturae : Literally "of caring". Translate: "in caring for people".
   ut hic . . . succurrat : "as for example this deity gives help . . ." The subjunctive is used to indicate that this is what people say.
46. *ille parturientibus dexter adsit :* "that one gives help to women in childbirth". *Parturientibus :* dative after the compound verb *adsit.*
49. *longissimum fuerit :* "it would be most boring".
   Sunt qui . . . valeant : "There are those who . . . have power". The subjunctive expresses the kind of deities being described, the class to which the deities belong.
56. *foret : = esset :* "would be".
58. *ut qui :* "as men who . . ." The subjunctives *consenescant, obsurdescant, contabescant* express the class to which the schoolteachers belong.
62. *meo beneficio :* "through my kindness".
65. *suo arbitratu :* "at their whim".
71. *puta :* See note to line 30 above.
75. *Quid autem cum . . . :* Literally: "What when . . ." Translate: "How shall I describe them when . . ."
76. *neque desunt qui mirentur :* The subjunctive expresses the class. Literally "Nor are there lacking such as admire".
77. *Maronis :* of Vergil, the great Roman poet (70–19 B.C.).
80. *hic :* literally "this man". The sense requires "another man".
81. *quae . . . tragoediae,* etc.: Understand some such verb as "result".
84. *annis plus viginti :* "for more than twenty years". *annis viginti,* ablative of comparison after *plus.*
85. *fore : = futurum esse. Se fore :* accusative and future infinitive introduced by the participle *ratus.*
   liceat, statuat : subjunctives in clauses in reported statement.
86. *distinguendae :* gerundive implying necessity.
   sint : subjunctive in the reported question introduced by *statuat.*
88. *Perinde quasi :* The framework of the sentence is: *res bello vindicanda sit si quis coniunctionem faciat . . .* A vague condition referring to the future with both verbs in the subjunctive. *Quasi* modifies the whole

phrase *res bello vindicanda sit*. Translate: "the matter would, as it were, have to be decided by war if anyone were to ... "

91. *Aldus :* Aldus Manutius (1450–1515), who founded the great Aldine printing press in Venice, was an intimate friend of Erasmus, published some of his writings, and gave him hospitality.
    meus : "my friend".

92. *dedit :* "gave to the world".
    hic : "our grammarian".
    nullam : Understand *grammaticam*.

93. *quam non evolvat :* "without going through it". The subjunctive is normal in indefinite or negative sentences of this type. Literally: "There is no grammar ... such as he does not ... "

94. *nemini non invidens :* "envying everyone".
    si quid ... moliatur : subjunctive as after verbs of fearing: "lest [or "in case"] he achieves ... "

95. *in hoc genere :* "in this type of work"—*i.e.* grammatical criticism and explanation.

97. *mea ... refert :* "it concerns me". *refert :* impersonal verb; *mea* Understand *re :* "my affair".

98. *magni :* "greatly", a genitive expressing the idea of value.
    modo fateamini : subjunctive with *modo* meaning "provided that".
    fieri : infinitive introduced by *fateamini*.

99. *eo :* "to that degree ... "

100. *cupiat :* subjunctive expressing consequence.
    neque : "not even".
    Persarum regibus : Persian kings were noted in ancient times for their vast wealth.

Text

Stultitiae Laus (ed. I. B. Kan; The Hague, 1898), Chapters 40, 41, and 49.

VOCABULARY

abbas, -atis, *m.*, abbot.
abicio, 3, abieci, abiectum, toss.
abominor, 1, *dep.*, dislike.
abscido, 3, -cidi, -cissum, cut off.
abscondo, 3, -condi, -conditum, hide from.
absque, *prep. with abl.*, deprived of.
abstinentia, -ae, *f.*, fasting.
abstineo, 2, -ui, -tentum, abstain.
accedo, 3, -cessi, -cessum, come to, be added to.
accendo, 3, -ndi, -nsum, light, encourage.
accingo, 3, -nxi, -nctum, surround, clothe, undergird.
accingor, gird oneself, make oneself ready.
accipio, 3, -cepi, -ceptum, take, receive.
acre, acris, acre, painful.
acies, -ei, *f.*, gaze, sight.
acroama, -atis, *n.*, musical entertainment.
actus, -us, *m.*, action.
addo, 3, -didi, -ditum, add.
adduco, 3, -duxi, -ductum, lead to.
adeo, besides, to such an extent.
adequito, 1, ride alongside.
adficio, 3, -feci, -fectum, torment, reward.
adfigo, 3, -ixi, -ixum, fix.
adfinis, -e, akin.
adfinitas, -atis, *f.*, relationship.
adflictus, -a, -um, wretched.

adfligo, 3, -ixi, -ictum, trouble.
adfulgeo, 2, adfulsi, appear.
adhuc, still.
adiaceo, 2, -ui, lie near.
adiutorium, -i, *n.*, tackle, assistance.
admitto, 3, -misi, -missum, adopt, admit.
admodum, sufficiently well.
admoneo, 2, -ui, -itum, warn.
adnavigo, 1, sail to.
adorno, 1, adorn.
adoro, 1, worship.
adquiro, 3, -quaesivi, -quaesitum, gain.
adsisto, 3, -stiti, -stitum, stand before.
adspiro, 1, blow.
adsto, 1, -stiti, stand near.
adsuesco, 3, -evi, -etum, become accustomed, accustom.
adsum, -esse, -fui, help.
adulatio, -onis, *f.*, worship.
adulescens, -entis, youthful.
adventus, -us, *m.*, arrival.
adversarius, -i, *m.*, rival.
adversum ⎫
adversus ⎬ *prep. with acc.*, against.
advolvo, 3, -vi, -utum, throw at the feet of.
aedes, -is, *f.*, temple.
aedificium, -i, *n.*, building.
aedifico, 1, build.
aedituus, -i, *m.*, priest.
Aegyptius, -a, -um, Egyptian.

aemulor, 1, *dep*., copy.
aeneus, -a, -um, made of brass.
aequalitas, -atis, *f*., excellent proportion.
aequo, 1, match.
aequor, -oris, *n*., sea, water.
aequus, -a, -um, equal.
aer, aeris, *m*., air.
aerumna, -ae, *f*., hardship.
aes, aeris, *n*., bronze.
aestas, -atis, *f*., summer.
aestimo, 1, reckon.
aestus, -us, *m*., heat.
aetas, -atis, *f*., age, generation.
aeternus, -a, -um, eternal.
aevum, -i, *n*., age.
africus, -i, *m*., south-west wind.
ager, -ri, *m*., land.
agito, 1, agitate, set in motion, drive.
agmen, -inis, *n*., column, company.
agnosco, 3, -novi, -nitum, recognize.
agnus, -i, *m*., lamb.
ago, 3, egi, actum, behave, do, render.
agrarius, -a, -um, agrarian.
aio, *defective verb*, say.
alacritas, -atis, *f*., readiness.
alatus, -a, -um, winged.
albeo, 2, be white.
albus, -a, -um, white.
alicubi, somewhere.
alienus, -a, -um, foreign.
aliquando, sometimes.
aliquantus, -a, -um, some.
aliquis, -quid, some, someone.
aliquot, several.
aliter, otherwise.
aliunde, from elsewhere.
alius, -a, -ud, other.
allevo, 1, lighten.
altare, -aris, *n*., altar.
alter, -era, -erum, the other, different.
altus, -a, -um, high.
alveus, -i, *m*., river-bed.
amaracinus, -a, -um, of marjoram.

ambio, 4, -ii, -itum, surround.
amicio, 4, -ixi, -itum, clothe.
amicitia, -ae, *f*., friendship.
amictus, -us, *m*., clothing.
amissio, -onis, *f*., loss.
amitto, 3, -misi, -missum, lose.
amplifico, 1, increase, spread.
amplius, more.
amplus, -a, -um, full.
anchorita, -ae, *m*., hermit.
ancora, -ae, *f*., anchor.
angelus, -i, *m*., angel.
Angli, -orum, *m*., Angles.
angustus, -a, -um, narrow.
anima, -ae, *f*., life, soul.
animaequus, -a, -um, bold.
animal, -alis, *n*., being.
animus, -i, *m*., heart, mind, courage.
annon, or not.
annona, -ae, *f*., allowance.
antea, previously.
antecedo, 3, -cessi, -cessum, precede.
anteferro, -ferre, -tuli, -latum, regard as superior.
antelucanus, -a, -um, before dawn.
antequam, before.
anterior, -ius, nearer to the front.
antiphona, -ae, *f*., response.
antiquus, -a, -um, ancient.
anulus, -i, *m*., ring.
apertilis, -e, easily opened.
apertus, -a, -um, clear.
apex, -icis, *m*., crown.
appareo, 2, -ui, -itum, appear.
appello, 1, address.
appendeo, 2, belong.
appetitus, -us, *m*., appetite.
appositus, -a, -um, appropriate.
approbo, 1, approve.
appropinquo, 1, approach.
aptus, -a, -um, suitable.
apud, *prep. with acc.*, with, among.
Aquaegrani, Aquarumgrani, Aachen (Aix-la-Chapelle).
Aquensis, -e, at, or of, Aquaegrani.
aquilo, -onis, *m*., north.

aquilonaris, -e, northern.
ara, -ae, f., altar.
arbitratus, -us, m., decision.
arbitrium, -i, n., wish.
arbitror, 1, dep., think.
arbor, -oris, f., tree, mast.
arca, -ae, f., chest.
ardeo, 2, arsi, arsum, burn.
arena, -ae, f., sand, shore, arena.
argentum, -i, n., silver.
arguo, 3, -ui, -utum, prove.
arma, -orum, n., weapons, warfare.
armamentum, -i, n., equipment.
arripio, 3, -ripui, -reptum, seize.
ars, artis, f., skill, pursuit.
artemon, -onis, m., foresail.
artifex, -icis, m., maker.
ascendo, 3, -di, -sum, climb, go on
    board.
asper, -era, -erum, rough, rocky.
aspicio, 3, -exi, -ectum, gaze at,
    behold.
assidue, regularly.
assuetus, -a, -um, accustomed.
assum, -i, n., roast meat.
astronomia, -ae, f., astronomy,
    astrology.
at, but.
atrium, -i, n., courtyard.
atrox, terrible.
attamen, and yet.
attenuo, 1, shorten.
attribuo, 3, -ibui, -ibutum, appor-
    tion.
auctor, -oris, m., creator.
auctoritas, -atis, f., impressiveness.
audeo, 2, ausus sum, dare.
aufero, -ferre, abstuli, ablatum,
    remove.
augeo, 2, auxi, auctum, increase.
aula, -ae, f., hall.
aura, -ae, f., wind.
aureus, -a, -um, golden.
auris, -is, f., ear.
aurum, -i, n., gold.
auster, -tri, m., south wind.
autem, and, but.

autumnus, -i, m., autumn.
autumo, 1, believe.
auxilior, 1, dep., help.
aversus, -a, -um, backwards.
averto, 3, -ti, -sum, turn away.
avis, -is, f., bird.
axis, -is, m., axle.

balneum, -i, n., bath.
bancus, -i, m., bench.
barba, -ae, f., beard.
barbare, badly.
barbaries, -ei, f., barbarian world.
barbarus, -a, -um, native.
barbatus, -a, -um, bearded.
basilica, -ae, f., cathedral.
beatus, -a, -um, blessed.
benedico, 3, -xi, -ctum, bless.
beneficium, -i, n., kindness.
benignus, -a, -um, kindly.
bestia, -ae, f., creature, animal.
bibo, 3, bibi, bibitum, drink.
biduum, -i, n., two days.
bifores, double doors.
biga, -ae, f., cart.
bigo, 1, travel by cart.
bini, -ae, -a, two each.
blandior, 4, delude oneself.
blasphemia, -ae, f., blasphemy.
bolis, -idis, f., sounding-lead.
bos, bovis m., ox.
bovinator, -oris, m., brawler.
breve, -is, n., document.
brevis, -e, short; brevi, in a short
    time.
bubsequa, -ae, m., herdsman.
bubulus, -a, -um, of an ox.
bulla, -ae, f., medallion.

cado, 3, cecidi, casum, fall.
caedes, -is, f., slaughter.
caedo, 3, cecidi, caesum, cut, beat.
caelestis, -e, heavenly.
caelibatus, -us, m., unmarried state.
caelum, -i, n., sky, heaven.
caesius, -a, -um, grey.
calamitosus, -a, -um, ill-fated,
    disastrous.

calciamentum, -i, *n.*, shoe.

calcio, 1, shoe.

caleo, 2, -ui, be warm.

calidus, -a, -um, warm.

calix, -icis, *m.*, chalice.

calor, -oris, *m.*, heat.

calvus, -a, -um, bald.

calx, calcis, *f.*, lime.

camela, -ae, *f.*, camel.

camera, -ae, *f.*, room.

cancellatus, -a, -um, interwoven.

cancellus, -i, *m.*, screen.

candela, -ae, *f.*, candle.

candor, -oris, *m.*, whiteness.

canities, -ei, *f.*, whiteness of hair.

canto, 1, chant, sing.

capillus, -i, hair.

capitaneus, -i, *m.*, regional commander.

capitulum, -i, *n.*, chapter, section.

capsa, -ae, *f.*, satchel.

caput, -itis, *n.*, head, end.

caracalla, -ae, *f.*, hooded cloak.

carcer, -eris, *m.*, prison.

careo, 2, -ui, -itum, go without.

caritas, -atis, *f.*, allowance.

carnalis, -e, physical, of the body.

carnifex, -icis, *m.*, executioner.

carnificina, -ae, *f.*, torture-chamber.

caro, carnis, *f.*, flesh.

carta, -ae, *f.*, paper, manuscript.

cartaceus, -a, -um, made of paper.

carus, -a, -um, dear.

castitas, -atis, *f.*, purity.

catena, -ae, *f.*, chain.

causa, -ae, *f.*, reason, means.

cedo, 3, cessi, cessum, yield, withdraw.

celebro, 1, celebrate.

cellarium, -i, *n.*, kitchen.

cellula, -ae, *f.*, cell.

celo, 1, conceal.

cena, -ae, *f.*, meal, dinner.

ceno, 1, dine.

censeo, 2, -ui, -um, consider.

cereolus, -i, *m.*, little candle.

certamen, -inis, *n.*, rivalry.

certe, at any rate.

certo, with certainty.

cervical, -alis, *n.*, cushion.

cervix, -icis, *f.*, neck.

cesso, 1, cease.

ceteri, -ae, -a, the rest.

ceterum, but.

character, -eris, *m.*, sign.

chorus, -i, *m.*, choir.

cingo, 3, -nxi, -nctum, encircle.

ciphus, -i, *m.*, cup, goblet.

circa, *prep. with acc.*, around.

circuitus, -us, *m.*, coast, circle, circumference.

circumfero, -ferre, -tuli, -latum, carry around.

circumlego, 3, -legi, -lectum, coast along.

circumsaepio, 4, -psi, -ptum, enclose.

cista, -ae, *f.*, chest.

cithara, -ae, *f.*, fiddle.

citharista, -ae, *m.*, fiddler, minstrel.

citra, beyond.

civilis, -e, civil.

civitas, -atis, *f.*, town, state.

clangor, -oris, *m.*, blast.

claritudo, -inis, *f.*, brilliance.

clarus, -a, -um, clear.

claudico, 1, limp.

claudo, 3, -si, -sum, end.

claudus, -a, -um, limping.

clepsydra, -ae, *f.*, water clock.

clericus, -i, *m.*, priest.

codicillus, -i, *m.*, notebook.

coeo, -ire, -ii, -itum, come together.

coepi, *defective*, begin.

coerceo, 2, -cui, -citum, confine.

cogitatio, -onis, *f.*, thought.

cogito, 1, plan.

cognomentum, -i, *n.*, surname.

cognosco, 3, -ovi, -itum, learn about.

collega, -ae, *m. or f.*, companion.

colloco, 1, place, allocate.

colloquor, 3, -locutus sum, *dep.*, converse.

89

collum, -i, *n.*, neck.

colo, 3, colui, cultum, worship, favour, study.

color, -oris, *m.*, colour.

coloro, 1, colour.

columna, -ae, *f.*, column.

colus, -i, *f.*, distaff.

comburo, 3, -ussi, -ustum, burn.

comedo, 3, -edi, -esum, eat together.

comes, -itis, *m. or f.*, companion, count.

commemoro, 1, relate.

comminiscor, 3, commentus sum, *dep.*, contrive.

committo, 3, -misi, -missum, begin, entrust.

commode, suitably.

commonefacio, 3, -feci, -factum, warn.

commoneo, 2, -ui, -itum, warn.

commoror, 1, -moratus sum, *dep.*, dwell.

commoveo, 2, -movi, -motum, move, stir up.

communio, -onis, *f.*, communion.

communis, -e, common.

commuto, 1, exchange.

comparo, 1, compare.

compeditus, -a, -um, fettered.

compello, 1, call to.

compello, 3, -puli, -pulsum, drive.

compenso, 1, make up for.

compes, -edis, *f.*, fetter.

compleo, 2, -evi, -etum, fulfil.

completorium, -i, *n.*, compline.

compono, 3, -posui, -positum, match.

compungo, 3, -nxi, -nctum, sting.

computo, 1, calculate.

condemno, 1, condemn.

condicio, -onis, *f.*, rank, situation.

condignus, -a, -um, worthy.

condonatio, -onis, *f.*, pardon, indulgence.

conduco, 3, -uxi, -uctum, lead.

confessor, -oris, *m.*, believer.

confestim, immediately.

conficio, 3, -feci, -fectum, make, wear out.

conflictus, -us, *m.*, conflict, clash.

confluo, 3, -fluxi, gather.

congredior, 3, -gressus sum, *dep.*, meet with.

congregatio, -onis, *f.*, community.

congrego, 1, collect.

congruo, 3, -ui, be in accord with.

congruus, -a, -um, suitable.

coniugium, -i, *n.*, marriage.

coniungo, 3, -nxi, -nctum, join.

conor, 1, *dep.*, try, make headway.

conscindo, 3, -idi, -issum, tear to pieces.

consenesco, 3, -nui, grow old.

consequenter, next.

consessus, -us, *m.*, seat.

considero, 1, look at, wonder.

consolor, 1, *dep.*, comfort, reassure.

consors, -ortis, *m. or f.*, sharer.

conspectus, -us, *m.*, sight.

conspicio, 3, -exi, -ectum, see.

constans, loyal.

constantia, -ae, *f.*, firmness.

constat, 1, -stitit, it is agreed.

constituo, 3, -ui, -utum, set up, situate.

construo, 3, -uxi, -uctum, build.

consultum, -i, *n.*, decision.

consummo, 1, complete.

consumo, 3, -mpsi, -mptum, use up.

contabesco, 3, -tabui, waste away.

contemptor, -oris, *m.*, despiser.

contentus, -a, -um, content.

continentia, -ae, *f.*, self-restraint.

contingo, 3, -tigi, -tactum, happen.

continuus, -a, -um, continual.

contionator, -oris, *m.*, mob-orator, preacher.

contionor, 1, *dep.*, harangue the mob.

contrarius, -a, -um, unfavourable.

contubernium, -i, *n.*, company.

convello, 3, -velli, -vulsum, uproot.

convenio, 4, -veni, -ventum, meet, confront, be fitting.

conversatio, -onis, *f.*, way of life.

converto, 3, -ti, -sum, turn, change.
convivor, 1, *dep.*, banquet.
cooperio, 4, -rui, -rtum, cover.
copiosus, -a, -um, rich.
cor, cordis, *n.*, heart.
coram, *prep. with abl.*, in the presence of.
corona, -ae, *f.*, crown.
corporalis, -e, physical.
corpus, -oris, *n.*, body, build.
corripio, 3, -ripui, -reptum, attack, influence.
corruo, 3, -ui, fall.
corus, -i, *m.*, north-west wind.
cotidianus, -a, -um, daily.
cotidie, daily.
creatura, -ae, *f.*, person, object.
creber, -bra, -brum, frequent.
crebro, frequently.
credo, 3, -didi, -ditum, believe, trust.
cremo, 1, burn.
crimen, -inis, *n.*, crime.
crinis, -is, *m.*, mane.
cristallum, -i, *n.*, crystal.
croceus, -a, -um, saffron-coloured.
cruciatus, -us, *m.*, pain.
crux, crucis, *f.*, cross.
cubo, 1, -ui, -itum, lie down.
cultus, -us, *m.*, worship, splendour, cultivation.
cum primum, as soon as.
cum . . . tum . . . , both . . . and . . .
cunctatio, -onis, *f.*, delay.
cunctus, -a, -um, all.
cupio, 3, -ivi, -itum, desire.
curia, -ae, *f.*, court, household.
curiosus, -a, -um, careful.
curo, 1, take care.
cursus, -us, *m.*, course.
custodia, -ae, *f.*, prisoner.
custos, -odis, *m. or f.*, guard.

daemon, -onis, *m.*, god.
damnum, -i, *n.*, loss.
Danuvius, -i, *m.*, Danube.
dea, -ae, *f.*, goddess.

debeo, 2, -ui, -itum, be bound to.
debilis, -e, feeble.
debitum, -i, *n.*, duty.
decedo, 3, -cessi, -cessum, die.
decennium, -i, *n.*, ten years.
decido, 3, -di, fall.
decollo, 1, behead.
decoro, 1, decorate.
decresco, 3, -crevi, -cretum, diminish.
decretum, -i, *n.*, rule.
decumbo, 3, -cubui, -cubitum, take to one's bed, lie ill.
decurro, 3, -cucurri, rush down, sail down.
dedecus, -oris, *n.*, shame.
defero, -ferre, -tuli, -latum, bear, pay, carry.
deficio, 3, -feci, -fectum, fail.
definio, 4, settle.
defunctus, -a, -um, dead.
deinceps, henceforth.
Deipara, giving birth to God.
delecto, 1, delight.
deleo, 2, -evi, -etum, destroy.
demereor, 2, -meritus sum, deserve earn.
demigro, 1, migrate.
denique, next, finally.
dens, dentis, *m.*, tooth.
deorsum, downwards.
depello, 3, -puli, -pulsum, drive off.
dependeo, 2, hang.
depono, 3, -posui, -positum, put aside.
deprecor, 1, *dep.*, pray.
deprehendo, 3, -di, -nsum, catch out.
deputo, 1, destine, allot.
derideo, 2, -si, -sum, mock.
descendo, 3, -di, -sum, disembark.
describo, 3, -psi, -ptum, lay out.
desero, 3, -ui, -tum, desert.
desertio, -onis, *f.*, depopulation.
deservio, 4, serve.
desideo, 2, -sedi, be inactive.
desidero, 1, wish, beg.

desino, 3, -sii, cease.
desponso, 1, marry.
destino, 1, appoint.
desum, -esse, -fui, be lacking.
desurgo, 3, rise.
deterior, -ius, worse.
deveho, 3, -vexi, -vectum, transport.
devenio, 4, -veni, -ventum, reach.
devinco, 3, -vici, -victum, subdue.
devito, 1, avoid.
devotio, -onis, f., consecration, devotion.
dexter, dextra, dextrum, favourable, helpful.
diaco, -onis, m., deacon
diadema, -atis, n., crown.
dialectica, -ae, f., philosophy.
dicaculus, -a, -um, talkative.
dictio, -onis, f., part of speech.
differo, -ferre, distuli, dilatum, put off.
digitus, -i, m., finger.
digladiatio, -onis, f., tearing to pieces, vicious onslaught.
dignor, 1, dep., deign
dilacero, 1, tear.
dilato, 1, open.
diligens, careful.
diligo, 3, -lexi, -lectum, love.
dimidium, -i, n., half.
dimitto, 3, -si, -ssum, set free, send away, set aside.
dira, -orum, n., woes.
dirigo, 3, -exi, -ectum, direct, raise.
discedo, 3, -cessi, -cessum, depart.
discerno, 3, -crevi, -cretum, distinguish.
discindo, 3, -cidi, -cissum, torment.
disciplina, -ae, f., education, practice.
disco, 3, -didici, learn.
discooperio, 4, -ui, -tum, uncover.
discrimen, -inis, n., danger, trial.
discrucio, 1, torture.
dissensio, -onis, f., discord.
distinguo, 3, -nxi, -nctum, mark, distinguish.

dithalassus, -a, -um, where two seas meet.
dives, -itis, rich.
divido, 3, -si, -sum, divide, separate.
divinator, -oris, m., prophet.
divinitas, -atis, f., divine nature, god.
divinitus, divinely.
divinus, -a, -um, divine.
divus, -i, m., god, divinity.
doctor, -oris, m., teacher.
doctus, -a, -um, learned.
documentum, -i, n., proof.
dolor, -oris, m., grief, suffering.
domina, -ae, f., lady.
dominica dies, Sunday.
domo, 1, -ui, -itum, conquer.
domuncula, -ae, f., miniature house.
domus, -us, f., home.
donec, until, while.
dono, 1, give.
dorsum, -i, back.
dubius, -a, -um, doubtful.
duntaxat, exactly, only.
duplex, -icis, double.
duro, 1, stretch.
durus, -a, -um, harsh.
dysenteria, -ae, f., dysentery.

ebrietas, -atis, f., drunkenness, bout of drunkenness.
ecce, behold.
ecclesia, -ae, f., church.
ecclesiasticus, -a, -um, ecclesiastic.
edisco, 3, -didici, learn.
edoceo, 2, -ui, -tum, instruct.
educo, 1, educate.
effodio, 3, -fodi, -fossum, dig out.
effugio, 3, -fugi, escape.
egredior, 3, egressus sum, dep., go out.
eiicio, 3, -eci, -ectum, cast, cast out.
eiulatus, -us, m., shrieking.
elegans, splendid.
elemosina, -ae, f., mercy.
elevo, 1, raise.

92

elixus, -a, -um, boiled.

eloquentia, -ae, *f.*, eloquence, speech.

emendo, 1, improve.

eminens, tall, high.

emineo, 2, -ui, stand out.

emitto, 3, -si, -ssum, cast out.

emollio, 4, -ii, -itum, soften.

enato, 1, swim ashore.

encomium, -i, *n.*, praise.

ensis, -is, *m.*, sword.

enumero, 1, list.

eo, ire, ii, itum, go.

eo quod, because.

equa, -ae, *f.*, mare.

equito, 1, ride.

erigo, 3, -rexi, -rectum, set up erect.

erro, 1, make a mistake.

error, -oris, *m.*, mistake.

erudio, 4, -ii, -itum, instruct.

etiam, also.

etsi, although.

euroaquilo, -onis, *m.*, north-easter.

evado, 3, -si, -sum, leave.

eveho, 3, -vexi, -vectum, carry.

evigilo, 1, keep awake.

evoco, 1, summon.

evolvo, 3, -volvi, -volutum, unroll and read.

exardesco, 3, -arsi, -arsum, break out

excedo, 3, -ssi, -ssum, exceed, break out.

excello, 3, -llui, -lsum, excel.

excidium, -i, *n.*, destruction.

excido, 3, -cidi, fall away.

excipio, 3, -cepi, -ceptum, exclude.

excito, 1, rouse.

excogito, 1, think up, devise.

excutio, 3, -cussi, -cussum, shake off, investigate.

exemplum, -i, *n.*, example.

exeo, -ire, -ii, -itum, leave.

exerceo, 2, -ui, -itum, train, practise.

exercito, 1, exercise.

exhibeo, 2, offer, support.

exhilaro, 1, enliven.

exhortatio, -onis, *f.*, exhortation.

exigo, 3, -egi, -actum, spend.

exiguus, -a, -um, small.

existimo, 1, think.

exitus, -us, *m.*, event.

exorior, 4, -ortus sum, *dep.*, arise.

exosus, -a, -um, hateful.

expedio, 4, -ii, -itum, carry out.

expergiscor, 3, -perrectus sum, *dep.*, wake up.

expers, having no share.

exprimo, 3, -pressi, -pressum, express.

expurgo, 1, cleanse.

exspecto, 1, wait.

exstinguo, 3, -nxi, -nctum, destroy, put out.

exstruo, 3, build up.

extendo, 3, -di, -tum, stretch out.

exterior, -ius, outer.

exterus, -a, -um, foreign.

extra, *adv. and prep. with acc.*, outside.

extraneus, -a, -um, outside, foreign.

extremitas, -atis, *f.*, end, corner.

extremus, -a, -um, last, rear.

exuberans, abounding.

exulto, 1, exult.

exuro, 3, -ussi, -ustum, burn away.

fabrico, 1, build.

facies, -ei, *f.*, face, countenance, complexion

facile, readily.

factum, -i, *n.*, deed.

facundus, -a, -um, eloquent.

fallo, 3, fefelli, falsum, deceive.

fama, -ae, *f.*, reputation.

famelicus, -a, -um, famished.

familia, -ae, *f.*, family.

famulus, -i, *m.* (famula, *f.*), servant.

farina, -ae, *f.*, material.

fateor, 2, fassus sum, *dep.*, confess.

fatigo, 1, weary.

fatum, -i, *n.*, disaster, death.

favilla, -ae, f., ash.
favor, -oris, m., acclamation, approval.
febris, is, f., fever.
felicitas, -atis, f., pleasure, happiness.
felix, fortunate.
fera, -ae, f., wild beast.
ferculum, -i, n., dish.
fere, almost.
ferio, 4, execute.
fero, ferre, tuli, latum, carry, bear.
ferrum, -i, n., iron, sword
ferula, -ae, f., whip.
festivitas, -atis, f., festival.
festum, -i, n., feast.
fetor, -oris, n., stench.
fictilis, -e, fashioned.
fides, -ei, f., faith.
fiducia, -ae, f., courage.
figuro, 1, fashion.
filiolus, -i, m., son.
filtrum, -i, n., felt.
findo, 3, fidi, fissum, split.
fingo, -nxi, -ctum, feign, invent.
finio, 4, finish.
fio, fieri, factus sum, become, happen, be made.
fixus, -a, -um, fixed.
flatus, -us, m., breeze.
flecto, 3, flexi, flexum, bend.
fleo, 2, flevi, fletum, weep.
fletus, -us m., weeping.
flo, 1, blow.
flos, floris, m., flower.
fluvius, -i, m., river.
fodio, 3, fodi, fossum, dig.
fons, fontis, m., spring, origin.
foras, forth.
forma, -ae, f., shape, presence, nature, type.
forte, perhaps, by chance.
fortis, -e, brave, violent.
fragmentum, -i, n., fragment.
frango, 3, -egi, -actum, break.
frequens, frequent.
frequento, 1, attend.

fretus, -a, -um, relying on.
frigidus, -a, -um, cold, lifeless.
frigus, -oris, n., cold.
frons, frontis, f., forehead, face, front.
fructuosus, -a, -um, fruitful.
fructus, -us, m., fruit.
fulgor, -oris, m., brightness, lightning.
fulguro, 1, flash with lightning.
fulmen, -inis, n., thunderbolt.
fulmino, 1, strike with lightning.
fumigatorium, -i, n., chimney.
fundo, 1, support.
fundo, 3, fudi, fusum, shed.
funereus, -a, -um, deadly.
funis, -is, m., rope.
funus, -eris, n., death.
furor, -oris, m., anger.
furtim, stealthily.
furtum, -i, n., theft.
fusus, -i, m., spindle.

gaudenter, joyfully.
gaudeo, 2, gavisus sum, rejoice.
gaudium, -i, n., joy.
gemmula, -ae, f., jewel.
genitus, -a, -um, born.
gens, gentis, f., people.
gentilicius, -a, -um, national, natural.
genuflecto, 3, -flexi, -flexum, kneel.
genu, -us, n., knee.
genus, -eris, n., type, race.
gero, 3, gessi, gestum, do.
gesto, 1, bear.
glorior, 1, dep., boast.
gradior, 3, gressus sum, dep., go.
grammatica, -ae, f,. literature, grammar.
grammaticus, -i, m., grammarian, schoolteacher.
graphium, -i, n., pencil.
gratia, -ae, f,. grace, thanks.
gravitas, -atis, f., solemnity.
gravo, 1, trouble.
gressus, -us, m., pace.

94

grex, gregis, *m.*, flock.
gubernaculum, -i, *n.*, steering-oar.
gubernator, -oris, *m.*, captain, helmsman.
guberno, 1, control.
gula, -ae, gullet.
gulosus, -a, -um, greedy.

habeo, 2, have, hold, regard.
habilis, -e, suitable.
habitudo, -inis, *f.*, appearance.
habitus, -us, *m.*, appearance, character, clothing.
hactenus, previously.
haedinus, -a, -um, of a kid.
haud dubie, without doubt.
haurio, 4, hausi, haustum, draw.
hebeto, 1, weaken.
herba, -ae, *f.*, plant, grass.
heres, -edis, *m. or f.*, heir.
hiemo, 1, winter.
hiems, -emis, *f.*, winter.
hilaris, -e, jovial.
hilaritas, -atis, *f.*, friendliness.
hinc et inde, on both sides.
historia, -ae, *f.*, history, story.
homicida, -ae, *m. or f.*, murderer.
honestas, -atis, *f.*, reverence.
honestus, -a, -um, proper.
honor, -oris, *m.*, honour, reward.
honoro, 1, honour.
horror, -oris, *m.*, dread.
hortor, 1, *dep.*, cheer.
hospitium, -i, *n.*, hospitality, hospital.
hospitor, 1, *dep.*, lodge.
hostia, -ae, *f.*, victim.
huc atque illuc, in all directions.
huiuscemodi, of this sort.
humanitas, -atis, *f.*, kindness.
humerus, -i, *m.*, shoulder.
humilitas, -atis, *f.*, humility.
hymnus, -i, *m.*, hymn.

iacto, 1, toss.
iactura, -ae, *f.*, loss.
iactus, -us, *m.*, throw, jettisoning.

ianitor, -oris, *m.*, attendant.
ibidem, in that very place.
idioma, -atis, *n.*, language.
idolatres, -ae, *m.*, idolater, worshipper of idols.
idolatria, -ae, *f.*, idolatry, shrine.
idolum, -i, *n.*, idol.
ieiunatio, -onis, *f.*, fast.
ieiunium, -i, *n.*, fast.
ieiunus, -a, -um, fasting.
igneus, -a, -um, fiery.
ignis, -is, *m.*, fire.
ignobilis, -e, low-born.
ignominia, -ae, *f.*, ill-repute.
ignoro, 1, be unacquainted with.
ignotus, -a, -um, unknown.
illicitus, -a, -um, forbidden.
illico, instantly.
imago, -inis, *f.*, image.
imber, -bris, *m.*, rain.
imbuo, 3, -ui, -utum, stain, instruct.
imitor, 1, *dep.*, imitate.
immensus, -a, -um, great.
immerito, unjustifiably.
immineo, 2, threaten.
immo, on the contrary, yes indeed, or rather.
immobilis, -e, firm.
impello, 3, -puli, -pulsum, drive on.
impendo, 3, -di, -sum, devote.
imperialis, -e, imperial.
impertio, 4, share, bestow.
impigre, zealously.
impingo, 3, -pegi, -pactum, run aground.
impius, -a, -um, wicked.
impono, 3, -posui, -positum, place on.
impostor, -oris, *m.*, cheat, impostor.
impostura, -ae, *f.*, deceit.
incedo, 3, -cessi, -cessum, walk.
incendo, 3, -di, -sum, light.
incessus, -us, *m.*, pace, gait.
inchoo, 1, begin.
incido, 3, -cidi, -casum, fall upon, chance upon.

95

incipio, 3, -cepi, -ceptum, begin.
inclino, 1, incline.
includo, 3, -usi, -usum, shut in, shut off.
incognitus, -a, -um, unknown.
incolumis, -e, safe.
incommodum, -i, *n.*, burden.
incorporalis, -e, spiritual.
incredibilis, -e, unusual.
increpo, 1, -ui -itum, rebuke.
inculco, 1, trample on.
incumbo, 3, -cubui, -cubitum, apply oneself.
incutio, 3, -cussi, -cussum, excite.
inde, from there
indecens, improper.
indecorus, -a, -um, immodest.
indico, 1, show.
indico, 3, -xi, -ctum, impose.
indignor, 1, *dep.*, be angry.
induo, 3, -ui, -utum, clothe, put on, adopt.
inedia, -ae, *f.*, fasting.
inepte, foolishly.
infamis, -e, notorious.
infantia, -ae, *f.*, childhood.
infelix, unhappy.
inferi, -orum, *m.*, the dead.
infernum, -i, *n.*, hell.
infero, -ferre, -tuli, illatum, lay, place, introduce.
infirmitas, -atis, *f.*, illness.
infra, *prep. with acc.*, inferior to.
infundo, 3, -fudi, -fusum, pour out.
ingredior, 3, ingressus sum, *dep.*, enter.
iniquitas, -atis, *f.*, injustice, evil.
initium, -i, *n.*, beginning.
iniungo, 3, -xi, -ctum, charge, enjoin.
iniuria, -ae, *f.*, damage, loss.
iniustus, -a, -um, unjust.
inlaesus, -a, -um, unharmed.
inludo, 3, -si, -sum, scorn, tease.
inquiro, 3, -sivi, -situm, hunt for.
inquisitio, -onis, *f.*, examination.
insania, -ae, *f.*, madness.

insigne, -is, *n.*, sign.
insinuo, 1, reveal, recommend, enjoin.
inspicio, 3, -exi, -ectum, gaze at.
inspiro, 1, inspire.
instinctus, -us, *m.*, inspiration.
instituo, 3, -ui, -utum, educate.
institutum, -i, *n.*, custom.
insulsus, -a, -um, tasteless, crude.
insum, -esse, -fui, be in.
insumo, 3, -mpsi, -mptum, use.
insuper, furthermore.
integer, -gra, -grum, pure, whole. de integro, afresh.
intellectus, -us, *m.*, mind.
intellego, 3, -exi, -ectum, understand.
intendo, 3, -di, -tum, consider.
intentio, -onis, *f.*, application.
interdico, 3, -xi, -ctum, forbid.
interfectio, -onis, *f.*, murder.
interim, sometimes.
interpositus, -a, -um, intervening.
interpres, -etis, *m.*, interpreter.
interpretor, 1, *dep.*, translate.
interrumpo, 3, -rupi, -ruptum, interrupt.
intersum, -esse, -fui, be present.
intra, *adv. and prep. with acc.*, within, before.
intrepidus, -a, -um, fearless.
intro, 1, enter.
introduco, 3, -xi, -ctum, bring in.
intromitto, 3, -si, -ssum, admit.
intueor, 2, intuitus sum, *dep.*, watch, gaze at.
invado, 3, -si, -sum, attack.
invectiva, -ae, *f.*, abuse.
invenio, 4, -ni, -ntum, find.
inventor, -oris, *m.*, discoverer.
invicem, one another, each other.
invideo, 2, -vidi, -visum, envy.
invisus, -a, -um, hateful.
invito, 1, invite.
involutus, -a, -um, in folds.
iracundia, -ae, *f.*, anger.
irrisio, -onis, *f.*, mockery.

irrito, 1, provoke.
Isiacus, -i, *m.*, devotee of Isis.
item, also, likewise.
iter, itineris, *n.*, journey.
itidem, also.
iucunditas, -atis, *f.*, pleasure, enjoyment.
iucundus, -a, -um, pleasurable.
iudex, -icis, *m.*, judge.
iudiciarius, -a, -um, judicial.
iudico, 1, judge, decide.
iumentum, -i, *n.*, ox.
iunctum, -i, *n.*, fastening.
iunctura, -ae, *f.*, fastening.
ius, iuris, *n.*, law.
iussum, -i, *n.*, order.
iussus, -us, *m.*, order.
iuxta, *adv. and prep. with acc.*, near.

labor, -i, lapsus sum, slip.
laboro, 1, strive.
lac, lactis, *n.*, milk.
lacrima, -ae, *f.*, tear.
lampas, -dis, *f.*, lamp.
lana, -ae, *f.*, wool.
languor, -oris, *m.*, weakness.
lanificium, -i, *n.*, working with wool.
lapis, -idis, *m.*, stone.
larva, -ae, *f.*, ghost.
lassitudo, -inis, *f.*, weariness.
lateo, 2, be hidden.
latitudo, -inis, *f.*, width.
latus, -eris, *n.*, side.
laus, laudis, *f.*, praise.
lautus, -a, -um, sumptuous.
lavo, 1, lavi, lautum, wash.
laxo, 1, loosen.
lectio, -onis, *f.*, reading, recital.
lector, -oris, *m.*, reader.
lectus, -i, *m.*, couch, litter.
lego, 3, legi, lectum, read, coast along.
lemures, -um, *m.*, spectres.
lentus, -a, -um, slow.
levis, -e, clean-shaven.
levo, 1, raise, lighten.
libens, willing.

liberalis, -e, liberal.
liberalitas, -atis, *f.*, generosity.
liberi, -orum, *m.*, children.
libertas, -atis, *f.*, freedom, independence.
libido, -inis, *f.*, lust.
licentia, -ae, *f.*, permission.
licet, 2, it is permitted.
ligneus, -a, -um, wooden.
ligo, 1, fasten.
linea, -ae, *f.*, line.
lingua, -ae, *f.*, language.
lis, litis, *f.*, quarrel, lawsuit.
litigo, 1, dispute.
litteratura, -ae, *f.*, writing.
litus, -oris, *n.*, shore, beach.
locutio, -onis, *f.*, speaking.
longaevus, -a, -um, long.
longitudo, -inis, *f.*, length.
loquor, 3, locutus sum, *dep.*, speak.
lorum, -i, *n.*, strap.
lucrum, -i, *n.*, profit.
luctus, -us, grief.
ludibrium, -i, *n.*, ridiculousness.
ludo, 3, -si, -sum, play, amuse oneself.
ludus, -i, *m.*, play.
lugeo, 2, -xi, -ctum, mourn.
lumen, -inis, *n.*, light.
luminar, -aris, *n.*, window, lamp.
luo, 3, -ui, pay.
lux, lucis, *f.*, light, dawn.
luxus, -us, *m.*, excess, luxury.

macilentus, -a, -um, lean.
magis, more.
magnanimitas, -atis, *f.*, greatness of heart.
magnificio, 3, -eci, -ectum, esteem highly.
magnitudo, -inis, *f.*, generosity.
maiestas, -atis, *f.*, majesty.
maior natu, older.
malo, malle, malui, prefer.
mālum, -i, *n.*, apple.
malum, -i, *n.*, harm, evil.
mamma, -ae, *f.*, breast, teat.

mandatum, -i, *n*., commandment, edict.
manduco, 1, eat.
mane, in the morning.
manens, settled.
mansio, -onis, *f*., dwelling.
mansionarius, -a, -um, lodging.
mansuetudo, -inis, *f*., gentleness.
manticulator, -oris, *m*., pickpocket.
margarita, -ae, *f*., pearl.
marmor, -oris, *n*., marble.
martyr, -yris, *m*., martyr.
martyrium, -i, *n*., martyrdom.
mas, maris, *m*., male, man.
matella, -ae, *f*., chamber pot.
materia, -ae, *f*., substance.
meatus, -us, *m*., course, channel.
medicus, -i, *m*., doctor.
mediocritas, -atis, *f*., average size.
medius, -a, -um, middle.
Melita, -ae, *f*., Malta.
mendacium, -i, *n*., lie.
mens, mentis, *f*., mind, spirit.
mensis, -is, *m*., month.
mensura, -ae, *f*., length.
mensuro, 1, measure.
merces, -edis, *f*., reward.
mereor, 2, meritus sum, *dep*., deserve.
meridianus, -a, -um, midday.
meridies, -ei, *m*., south.
meritus, -a, -um, deserved.
merus, -a, -um, pure.
metallum, -i, *n*., metal.
metior, 4, mensus sum, measure out.
metor, 1, *dep*., lay out.
metuo, 3, -ui, -utum, fear.
militia, -ae, *f*., warfare.
minae, -arum, *f*., threats.
minax, threatening.
minime, very little.
minister, -tri, *m*., server.
ministerium, -i, *n*., service.
ministro, 1, serve.
minor, 1, *dep*., threaten.
minuo, 3, -ui, -utum, lessen.

minus, less.
mirabilis, -e, incredible.
miraculum, -i, miracle.
miror, 1, *dep*., marvel, be surprised, admire.
mirus, -a, -um, wonderful.
misceo, 2, miscui, mixtum, mingle.
miser, -era, -erum, ill-fated, wretched.
missa, -ae, *f*., mass.
mitigo, 1, soften.
mitto, 3, -si, -ssum, send, hurl, let down.
mixtim, alternately.
modicus, -a, -um, small.
modo, now, only.
modus, -i, *m*., manner, extent, custom.
moleste, offensively.
molior, 4, accomplish.
monachus, -i, *m*., monk.
monasterium, -i, *n*., monastery.
mora, -ae, *f*., delay.
morbus, -i, *m*., sickness.
morio, -onis, *m*., fool, jester.
mors, mortis, *f*., death.
mortalis, -e, human.
mortuus, -a, -um, dead.
mos, moris, *m*., custom.
motus, -us, *m*., movement.
mulier, -eris, *f*., woman.
muliercula, -ae, *f*., woman.
multiplico, 1, increase.
multitudo, -inis, *f*., crowd, quantity.
munditia, -ae, *f*., cleanliness, thing of elegance.
mundus, -i, *m*., world, universe.
mungo, 3, milk.
munusculum, -i, *n*., little reward.
mutilus, -a, -um, mutilated.
mutuus, -a, -um, mutual.
mysterium, -i, *n*., mystery.

nasus, -i, *m*., nose.
natatus, -us, *m*., swimming.
natio, -onis, *f*., people.

nativitas, -atis, f., birth.
nato, 1, swim.
natura, -ae, f., form, natural course.
naturaliter, naturally.
nauclerus, -i, m., ship-owner.
naufragium, -i, n., shipwreck.
navigatio, -onis, f., sailing.
ne . . . quidem, not even.
nebulo, -onis, m., booby.
necdum, not yet.
necessarius, -a, -um, necessary.
necesse, necessary.
necessitas, -atis, f., necessity.
nedum, much more.
nefandus, -a, -um, wicked.
negotiator, -oris, m., businessman.
negotium, -i, n., duty.
nepos, -otis, m., grandson.
neptis, -is, f., grand-daughter.
nequaquam, not at all.
neutiquam, by no means.
nimirum, clearly.
nimius, -a, -um, extreme.
nitor, -oris, m., luxuriance.
niveus, -a, -um, snowy.
nix, nivis, f., snow.
nobilitas, atis, f., nobility.
noctu, by night.
nocturnus, -a, -um, of the night.
nolo, nolle, nolui, be unwilling.
nomen, -inis, n., name.
nonnunquam, sometimes.
nosco, 3, novi, notum, know.
noto, 1, mark.
notula, -ae, f., little mark.
novitas, -atis, f., unusualness.
noxius, -a, -um, harmful.
nubes, -is, f., cloud.
nucleus, -i, m., nut shell.
nugamentum, -i, n., plaything.
numen, -inis, n., god.
numero, 1, count.
numerus, -i, m., number.
nummus, -i, m., coin.
nusquam, nowhere.
nutrio, 4, feed.
nutus, -us, m., will.

obeo, -ire, -ii, -itum, visit.
obesus, -a, -um, fat.
obitus, -us, m., death.
obnoxius, -a, -um, liable to.
obsequium, -i, n., escort, obedience.
obstaculum, -i, n., obstacle.
obsurdesco, 3, -dui, become deaf.
obtentus, -us, m., pretence.
obtineo, 2, -ui, -tentum, secure.
obtutus, -us, m., gaze.
obviam, face to face; obviam eo,
    meet.
occasio, -onis, f., opportunity.
occidentalis, -e, western.
occido, 3, -di, -sum, kill.
occupo, 1, fill.
occurro, 3, -curri, -cursum, meet,
    come to meet.
ocius, quickly.
oculatus, -a, -um, keen-eyed.
oculus, -i, m., eye.
offensio, -onis, f., affront, insult.
offero, -ferre, obtuli, oblatum,
    offer.
officium, -i, n., duty, service, office.
omitto, 3, -misi, -missum, give up.
onerosus, -a, -um, burdensome.
onus, oneris, n., cargo.
opera, -ae, f., attention.
operio, 4, -ui, -tum, cover.
opes, -um, f., wealth.
operor, 1, dep., make.
opifex, -icis, m. or f., workman.
opinor, 1, dep., think.
oportet, 2, -uit, it behoves, is neces-
    sary.
oppono, 3, -sui, -situm, set before.
opprimo, 3, -pressi, -pressum,
    crush.
optimates, -ium, m., nobles.
opto, 1, wish, pray.
opus, -eris, n., work, workmanship.
oratio, -onis, f., prayer, speech.
oratorium, -i, n., place of prayer.
orbis, -is, m., circle, globe, round.
ordinate, in order.
ordino, 1, station.

ordo, -inis, *m.*, rank, row, class.
orientalis, -e, eastern.
origo, -inis, *f.*, origin.
orno, 1, adorn.
oro, 1, pray.
ortus, -us, *m.*, rising.
os, oris, *n.*, mouth, lip.
os, ossis, *n.*, bone.
osculor, 1, *dep.*, kiss.
ostendo, 3, -di, -tum, display, depict.
ostento, 1, vaunt.
ostiolum, -i, *n.*, small door.
ostium, -i, *n.*, doorway.
otiosus, -a, -um, unemployed.
otium, -i, *n.*, idleness.

pactio, -onis, *f.*, bargain.
pactum, -i, *n.*, agreement.
paedor, -oris, *m.*, filth.
paganus, -a, -um, heathen.
palam, openly.
palatium, -i, *n.*, palace.
pallium, -i, *n.*, cloak.
pannus, -i, *m.*, garment.
par, equal.
parco, 3, peperci, parsum, spare.
parcus, -a, -um, sparing.
parens, -entis, *m. or f.*, parent.
pareo, 2, obey.
paries, -etis, *m.*, wall.
pario, 3, peperi, partum, produce.
pariter, equally.
pars, partis, *f.*, direction.
partim, partly.
partior, 4, share out.
parturio, 4, bring forth.
parum, little.
parvulus, -a, -um, quite small, young.
pasco, 3, pavi, pastum, lead to pasture.
pascua, -orum, *n.*, pasture lands.
pascuolus, -a, -um, suitable for grazing.
passim, everywhere.
passus, -us, *m.*, fathom, track.

patienter, patiently.
patientia, -ae, *f.*, endurance.
patina, -ae, *f.*, paten, dish.
patior, 3, passus sum, *dep.*, allow, suffer.
patrius, -a, -um, native.
paulatim, gradually.
paululum, a little.
pauper, poor.
pavidus, -a, -um, fearful.
pax, pacis, *f.*, peace.
pectus, -oris, *n.*, breast, chest.
peculiarius, -a, -um, particular.
peior, -ius, worse.
pelagus, -i, *n.*, sea.
pellicula, -ae, *f.*, skin.
pendeo, 2, pependi, hang.
penes, *prep. with acc.*, with.
per, *prep. with acc.*, through, by means of.
perago, 3, -egi, -actum, spend, commit.
percello, 3, -culi, -culsum, strike.
percenseo, 2, -censui, -censum, go through.
percipio, 3, -cepi, -ceptum, receive.
percussor, -oris, *m.*, murderer.
percutio, 3, -cussi, -cussum, execute.
perdo, 3, -didi, -ditum, destroy, lose.
perduco, 3, -xi, -ctum, lead, bring.
peregrinor, 1, *dep.*, travel.
peregrinus, -i, *m.*, foreigner.
perennis, -e, continual, ever-flowing.
pereo, -ire, -ii, -itum, perish, be harmed.
perfero, -ferre, -tuli, -latum, suffer.
perfidus, -a, -um, heathen.
perfinio, 4, finish.
perfruor, 3, perfructus sum, *dep.*, enjoy.
pergo, 3, perrexi, perrectum, proceed.
perhibeo, 2, -ui, -itum, report.
periculosus, -a, -um, dangerous.
perinde, just as.

peritus, -a, -um, skilled.
periurium, -i, n., false oath.
permaneo, 2, -si, -sum, remain.
permuto, 1, change.
perniciosus, -a, -um, disastrous.
perperam, wrongly.
perpetim, continually.
perpetuo, continually.
perpetuus, -a, -um, continuous.
persecutio, -onis, f., persecution.
persecutor, -oris, m., persecutor.
persentio, 4, -si, -sum, perceive.
persequor, 3, -secutus sum, *dep.*, prosecute.
persevero, 1, persevere, continue.
persolvo, 3, -vi, -utum, perform.
persuasio, -onis, f., belief.
pertica, -ae, f., pole.
pertineo, 2, -ui, concern, lead to, appertain to.
pertraho, 3, -axi, -actum, drag to trial.
pervenio, 4, -veni, -ventum, reach.
peto, 3, -ivi, -itum, ask for.
phalerae, -arum, f., trappings (for horses).
pharetra, -ae, f., quiver.
pictus, -a, -um, painted.
pietas, -atis, f., holiness, kindness, devotion.
pistrina, -ae, f., grinding mill.
pius, -a, -um, holy.
placeo, 2, please.
planctus, -us, m., wailing.
plane, clearly.
plango, 3, -nxi, -nctum, bewail.
planus, -a, -um, flat.
platea, -ae, f., main street.
plaudo, 3, -si, -sum, clap.
plebs, plebis, f., people.
plecto, 3, punish, execute.
plenus, -a, -um, full.
plerique, -aeque, -aque, very many.
plumarium opus, feather stitch.
plurimus, -a, -um, very much, very many.
plus, more, several.

poena, -ae, f., punishment.
polimitarium opus, embroidery.
polliceor, 2, promise.
polluo, 3, -ui, -utum, dishonour.
pondus, -eris, n., weight.
pone, behind.
pontifex, -icis, m., pope.
popularis, -e, of the people.
porrigo, 3, -rexi, -rectum, hold out.
porro, onward, then, moreover.
portentosus, -a, -um, strange.
portus, -us, m., harbour.
posco, 3, poposci, require.
possideo, 2, -edi, -essum, own.
possum, posse, potui, be able.
postea, afterwards.
posteaquam, after.
posticium, -i, n., back-door.
postremo, finally.
postulo, 1, ask.
potestas, -atis, f., power, magistrate.
potius, rather.
poto, 1, drink.
potus, -us, m., drink.
prae, *prep. with abl.*, because of.
praebeo, 2, provide.
praecedo, 3, -ssi, -ssum, precede.
praeceptor, -oris, m., teacher.
praeceptum, -i, n., instruction.
praecipio, 3, -epi, -eptum, order.
praecipue, especially.
praecipuus, -a, -um, special.
praeclarus, -a, -um, excellent.
praedestinatio, -onis, f., forethought.
praedium, -i, n., estate.
praefatus, -a, -um, previously mentioned.
praeficio, 3, -feci, -fectum, appoint.
praegrandis, -e, very large.
praeparo, 1, prepare.
praepolleo, 2, be very powerful.
praeposterus, -a, -um, at the wrong time, out of season.
praeripio, 3, -ripui, -reptum, snatch (before another).
praescriptus, -a, -um, prescribed.

praesens, present.
praesertim, especially.
praesto, at hand.
praesto, 1, -iti, -itum, offer, show, fulfil.
praesum, -esse, -fui, be in charge.
praesumo, 3, -mpsi, -mptum, dare, presume.
praeter, *prep. with acc.*, except.
praetereo, -ire, -ii, -itum, pass.
praetermitto, 3, -misi, -missum, omit.
praeterquam, except.
praeterquod, except that.
praetitulo, 1, entitle.
prandium, -i, *n.*, midday meal.
precula, -ae, *f.*, little prayer.
premo, 3, -essi, -essum, afflict.
pretiosus, -a, -um, precious.
prima, -ae, *f.*, main place.
primogenitus, -a, -um, eldest.
primor, -oris, *m.*, noble.
princeps, -ipis, *m.*, headman, magistrate, emperor.
prior, -ius, earlier.
privatus, -a, -um, personal.
pro, *prep. with abl.*, for, on behalf of, instead of.
procedo, 3, -essi, -essum, come forth.
proceritas, -atis, *f.*, height.
procuro, 1, provide.
prodigiosus, -a, -um, about the future.
proditio, -onis, *f.*, betrayal.
prodo, 3, -idi, -itum, proclaim.
produco, 3, -xi, -ctum, spend.
profecto, assuredly.
professor, -oris, *m.*, teacher.
proficio, 3, -feci, -fectum, profit.
proficiscor, 3, profectus sum, *dep.*, set out.
prohibeo, 2, hinder, prevent.
proicio, 3, -ieci, -iectum, throw down, jettison.
proiectus, -a, -um, protruding.
promiscuus, -a, -um, common,

general.
promitto, 3, -misi, -missum, promise.
pronuntio, 1, proclaim, speak.
prope, almost.
propemodum, almost.
propono, 3, -sui, -situm, set before.
propositum, -i, *n.*, intention.
propter, *prep. with acc.*, because of, in view of.
propterea quod, because.
prora, -ae, *f.*, prow.
prosper, propitious.
prosperus, -a, -um, sound.
prorsus, wholly.
prospicio, 3, -exi, -ectum, provide.
prosterno, 3, -stravi, -stratum, prostrate.
protinus, immediately.
prout, according as.
provincia, -ae, *f.*, area.
provoco, 1, provoke.
proximus, -a, -um, very near.
pruritus, -us, *m.*, desire.
psallo, 3, -i, chant.
publice, in public.
pudet me, I am ashamed.
pueritia, -ae, *f.*, childhood.
puerulus, -i, *m.*, little boy.
pulchritudo, -inis, *f.*, beauty.
pulso, 1, knock.
pulvis, -eris, *m.*, dust.
puppa, -ae, *f.*, doll.
puppis, -is, *f.*, stern, ship.
purgatorium, -i, *n.*, purgatory.
pusillum, a little.
puter, -tris, -tre, decaying.
pyra, -ae, *f.*, fire.
pyramis, -idis, *f.*, pyramid.

quadrangulus, -i, *m.*, square basket.
quadratus, -a, -um, square.
quaero, 3, -sivi, -itum, seek, ask for.
quaestio, -onis, *f.*, inquiry.
quaestus, -us, *m.*, gain.
qualiscunque, qualecunque, anyone at all.

quamdiu, as long as.
quamquam, although.
quamvis, although.
quandoquidem, since.
quantitas, -atis, f., size.
quanto magis, how much more.
quantumlibet, however, however much.
quantumvis, however, however much.
quapropter, accordingly.
quare, why.
quasi, as if.
quater, four times.
quaterni, -ae, -a, four each.
quemadmodum, just as.
queo, -ire, -ii, -itum, be able.
queror, 3, questus sum, dep., complain.
quia, because, that.
quicunque, whoever.
quidam, quaedam, quoddam, a certain.
quidem, really, in truth; ne . . . quidem, not even.
quiesco, 3, -evi, -etum, rest.
quilibet, anyone.
quin, indeed, in fact.
quinquies, five times.
quippe, inasmuch as.
quispiam, someone.
quisquam, anyone.
quisque, each.
quisquis, whoever.
quivis, anyone.
quoad, as far as.
quo facto, whereupon.
quo modo, how, somehow.
quondam, formerly.
quoniam, since, that.
quoties, whenever.

radius, -i, m., ray.
radix, -icis, f., vegetable.
rado, 3, -si, -sum, shave.
rapidus, -a, -um, swift.
rapina, -ae, f., theft.

rapio, 3, -ui, -tum, abduct.
raro, rarely.
ratio, -onis, f., reason, regard.
ratiocinor, 1, dep., reason, argue.
ratus, -a, -um, thinking.
rebellis, -e, rebel.
recedo, 3, -ssi, -ssum, depart.
receptio, -onis, f., shelter.
recipio, 3, -epi, -eptum, receive, welcome.
recito, 1, recite.
recolo, 3, -colui, -cultum, recollect.
recondo, 3, -idi, -itum, bury.
recreo, 1, amuse.
recuso, 1, refuse.
reddo, 3, -idi, -itum, surrender, pay.
redeo, -ire, -ii, -itum, return.
redimo, 3, -emi, -emptum, atone.
refectio, -onis, f., refreshment.
refectorium, -i, n., refectory.
refero, -ferre, -tuli, -latum, repay.
reficio, 3, -feci, -fectum, refresh.
regia, -ae, f., palace.
regio, -onis, f., place.
regnum, -i, n., kingdom, rule, royal power.
religio, -onis, f., religion.
religiose, with devotion.
reliquus, -a, -um, remaining.
remuneratio, -onis, f., reward.
repleo, 2, -evi, -etum, fill.
repromitto, 3, -si, -ssum, promise.
requiesco, 3, -evi, -etum, rest.
res, rei, f., event, history, action, property.
resideo, 2, -sedi, remain.
resilio, 4, -ui, jump back.
respicio, 3, -exi, -ectum, face.
responsum, -i, n., reply.
restis, -is, f., cord.
restituo, 3, -tui, -tutum, restore.
retineo, 2, -ui, -tentum, keep, maintain.
retraho, 3, -xi, -ctum, remove.
reus, rea, responsible.
revelatio, -onis, f., revelation.
revelo, 1, reveal.

reverens, reverent.
reverentia, -ae, *f.*, reverence.
revertor, 3, reversus sum, *dep.*,
   return.
revoco, 1, recall.
rhetorica, -ae, *f.*, rhetoric.
ridiculus, -a, -um, ridiculous.
rimor, 1, *dep.*, investigate.
ritus, -us, *m.*, rite, ceremony, function.
rixa, -ae, *f.*, quarrel.
robustus, -a, -um, sturdy.
rota, -ae, *f.*, wheel, circle.
rotundus, -a, -um, round.
rubus, -i, *m.*, bush.
rursus (*and* rursum), again.

sacer, -ra, -rum, sacred; *nom. plu.*,
   sacra, rites.
sacerdos, -otis, *m.*, priest.
sacerdotalis, -e, priestly.
sacramentum, -i, *n.*, sacred mystery.
sacrificium, -i, *n.*, sacrifice, sacra-
   ment.
sacrifico, 1, sacrifice.
sacrificus, -i, *m.*, priest.
sacrilegus, -i, *m.*, unbeliever.
saeculum, -i, *n.*, century.
saevio, 4, rage.
saevus, -a, -um, wild.
sagax, wise.
salto, 1, dance.
salus, -utis, *f.*, safety, greeting.
salutaris, -e, saving.
saluto, 1, greet.
salvo, 1, heal.
salvus, -a, -um, safe.
sanctifico, 1, consecrate.
sanctus, -a, -um, saintly, holy,
   devoted.
sanguis, -inis, *m.*, blood.
sapor, -oris, *m.*, flavour.
sarmentum, -i, *n.*, brushwood.
satelles, -itis, *m. or f.*, attendant.
satietas, -atis, *f.*, over-abundance.
satio, 1, satisfy, fill.
saturitas, -atis, *f.*, abundance.

scamnum, -i, *n.*, bench.
scapha, -ae, *f.*, boat.
scelus, -eris, *n.*, crime.
schola, -ae, *f.*, school.
sculptus, -a, -um, sculptured.
scurrilitas, -atis, *f.*, buffoonery,
   thoughtlessness.
secretus, -a, -um, hidden.
secta, -ae, *f.*, sect.
secundum, *prep. with acc.*, in accordance with.
sedile, -is, *n.*, seat.
seditio, -onis, *f.*, riot, civil war.
sedulo, diligently.
segnitia, -ae, *f.*, idleness.
semel, once, once for all.
senecta, -ae, *f.*, old age.
senectus, -utis, *f.*, old age.
senior, elder.
sententia, -ae, *f.*, decision.
separo, 1, separate.
sepultura, -ae, *f.*, burial.
sequor, 3, secutus sum, *dep.*, follow.
serenitas, -atis, *f.*, peace.
sereno, 1, be calm, clear.
sericus, -a, -um, silken.
sermo, -onis, *m.*, discourse.
sero, late.
servilis, -e, slave, of a slave.
servitus, -us, *m.*, slavery.
servo, 1, save.
sescenti, -ae, -a, innumerable.
sexagenarius, -i, *m.*, sexagenarian,
   man of sixty years.
sexus, -us, *m.*, sex.
sicco, 1, dry.
sicut, as.
sidus, -eris, *n.,* star.
sigillatim, one at a time.
signum, -i, *n.*, signal.
similiter, likewise.
simul, at the same time.
simulacrum, -i, *n.*, image.
sine, *prep. with abl.*, without.
singulariter, exceedingly.
singuli, -ae, -a, individuals, particular.

sino, 3, -vi, -tum, allow.
sive, or.
socius, -i, *m.*, companion.
soleo, 2, solitus sum, be accustomed.
solitus, -a, -um, usual.
sollemnis, -e, customary.
sollemniter, solemnly.
solum, only.
solvo, 3, -vi, -utum, break up, un-
fasten, pay.
somnus, -i, *m.*, sleep.
sordes, is, *f.*, filthy surroundings.
sordidus, -a, -um, base, cheap, dirty,
poor.
sors, sortis, *f.*, lot, destiny.
sortilegium, -i, *n.*, divination, for-
tune-telling.
spargo, 3, -si, -sum, sprinkle,
spread, scatter.
spatium, -i, *n.*, distance, duration.
species, -iei, *f.*, appearance.
spectrum, -i, *n.*, apparition.
speculator, -oris, *m.*, spectator.
spes, spei, *f.*, hope.
spiritalis, -e, spiritual.
spiritus, -us, *m.*, spirit.
splendeo, 2, shine.
spontanee, willingly.
sponte, *abl.f.*, of one's own accord.
stadium, -i, *n.*, furlong.
statuo, 3, -ui, -utum, agree on.
statura, -ae, *f.*, stature.
status, -a, -um, appointed.
statuuncula, -ae, *f.*, small statue.
stirps, stirpis, *f.*, family, stock.
strages, -is, *f.*, slaughter.
strepitus, -us, *m.*, sound, noise.
stringo, 3, -inxi, -ictum, draw,
draw tight.
structura, -ae, *f.*, building.
studeo, 2, devote oneself to.
studiosus, -a, -um, eager.
studium, -i, *n.*, pursuit, enthusiasm.
stultitia, -ae, *f.*, stupidity.
suave, persuasively.
suavis, -e, sweet.
subeo, -ire, -ii, -itum, undergo.

subiectus, -a, -um, devoted.
subinde, thereupon.
submissim, in a low voice.
subnavigo, 1, sail in the lee of.
subsisto, 3, -stiti, stay.
succedo, 3, -ssi, -ssum, follow, suc-
seed, take the place of.
succendo, 3, -di, -sum, inflame.
succinctus, -a, -um, tucked up.
succurro, 3, -curri, -cursum, help.
summitas, -atis, *f.*, top.
summitto, 3, -si, -ssum, lower.
summoveo, 2, -vi, -tum, take away.
supellex, -lectilis, *f.*, goods.
super, *adv. and prep. with acc.*, on,
after.
superi, -orum, *m.*, the gods.
superius, higher.
supernus, -a, -um, of heaven.
superstes, surviving.
supersum, -esse, -fui, be left.
supervenio, 4, -ni, -ntum, arrive.
suppeto, 3, -ivi, -itum, be available.
supplicium, -i, *n.*, torture.
supplicor, 1, *dep.*, make supplication.
suppositio, -onis, *f.*, substitution.
sursum, upwards.
suscipio, 3, -cepi, -ceptum, welcome.
suspendo, 3, -di, -sum, hang.
suspicor, 1, *dep.*, suspect, believe.
sustento, 1, sustain.
sustineo, 2, -ui, -tentum, bear.

tabula, -ae, *f.*, plank, tablet.
taedium, -i, *n.*, boredom.
talio, -onis, *f.*, retaliation.
tamquam, as if.
tantum, so much, only.
temere, heedlessly.
temperans, temperate.
tempestas, -atis, *f.*, storm.
tempto, 1, try.
tempus, -oris, *n.*, time.
tendo, 3, tetendi, tentum, make
one's way.
tenebrae, -arum, *f.*, darkness.

teneo, 2, -ui, -tum, hold, keep to, grasp, achieve.
ter, three times.
terminus, -i, *m.*, boundary.
tero, 3, trivi, -tritum, stamp.
terrenus, -a, -um, of the earth.
terricula, -ae, *f.*, terror.
territo, 1, terrify.
testis, -is, *m. or f.*, witness.
testudo, -inis, *f.*, arch.
thesaurus, -i, *m.*, treasure.
tiara, -ae, *f.*, head-dress.
tignum, -i, *n.*, beam, main support.
timor, -oris, *m.*, fear.
titillo, 1, captivate.
tollo, 3, sustuli, sublatum, raise, take away.
tono, 1, -ui, thunder.
tormentum, -i, *n.*, torment, torture.
torpeo, 2, be idle.
torqueo, 2, torture.
torques, -is, *f.*, necklace.
torrens, -entis, *m.*, torrent.
tortor, -oris, *m.*, torturer.
tot, so many.
totidem, so many.
totum, wholly.
tracto, 1, treat.
tractus, -us, *m.*, movement.
trado, 3, -didi, -ditum, hand on, hand over.
traho, 3, -xi, -ctum, drag, drive.
transeo, -ire, -ii, -itum, cross.
transpono, 3, -sui, -situm, transfer.
transvado, 1, ford.
tribunal, -alis, *n.*, court.
tribuo, 3, -ui, -utum, give, attribute.
triduo, for three days.
trini, -ae, -a, three each.
Trinitas, -atis, *f.*, Trinity.
triticum, -i, *n.*, grain.
triumpho, 1, triumph.
tuba, -ae, *f.*, trumpet.
tueor, 2, tuitus sum, *dep.*, protect.
tugurium, -i, *n.*, cottage.
tumor, -oris, *m.*, swelling.
tumultus, -us, *m.*, riot.

turba, -ae, *f.*, crowd.
turbidus, -a, -um, turbid, muddy.
turbo, 1, disturb.
turma, -ae, *f.*, company.
typhonicus, -a, -um, tempestuous.

uber, -eris, *n.*, breast, udder.
ubique, everywhere.
ultimus, -a, -um, last, lowest.
ultio, -onis, *f.*, vengeance.
ultro, voluntarily.
una cum, together with.
unanimiter, with one accord.
unde, from where.
undecunque, from all parts.
undique, all around.
ungulatus, -a, -um, hooved.
unicus, -a, -um, only, single.
universus, -a, -um, altogether, all, whole.
unusquisque, each.
Urbs, Urbis, *f.*, Rome.
urceolus, -i, *m.*, ewer, jug.
uro, 3, ussi, ustum, burn.
usque ad, as far as.
uter, utris, *m.*, skin, bag.
uterque, -traque, -trumque, each.
utinam, Oh that . . . , would that . . .
utique, certainly.
utor, 3, usus sum, *dep.*, use.
uxor, -oris, *f.*, wife.

vacca, -ae, *f.*, cow.
vaccinus, -a, -um, of a cow.
vaco, 1, have time.
vacuus, -a, -um, unoccupied.
vado, 3, go.
vagor, 1, *dep.*, roam, range.
valde, very.
valeo, 2, -ui, -itum, be able.
valetudo, -inis, *f.*, health.
validus, -a, -um, violent.
vapor, -oris, *m.*, vapour.
varietas, -atis, *f.*, variety.
vario, 1, adorn.
vas, vasis, *n.*, vessel, equipment.
vasculum, -i, *n.*, vessel.

vastitas, -atis, f., devastation.
vectura, -ae, f., traffic.
vegetus, -a, -um, lively.
vehementer, violently.
velut, or veluti, as if.
venator, -oris, m., hunter.
venatrix, -icis, f., huntress.
venatus, -us, m., hunting.
veneror, 1, dep., respect, worship.
venor, 1, dep., hunt.
venter, -tris, m., stomach, paunch.
ver, veris, n., spring.
verber, -eris, n., blow.
verbulum, -i, n., petty word.
verecundia, -ae, f., humility.
veritas, -atis, f., truth.
vero, but, however, indeed.
versicolor, many-coloured.
versiculum, -i, n., verse, little verse.
versus, -us, m., verse.
versus, adv. and prep. with acc., to-
    wards.
vertex, -icis, m., summit.
verto, 3, -ti, -sum, turn.
veru, -us, n., spit, skewer.
verum, but.
verus, -a, -um, true.
vescor, 3, dep., feed.
vesper, -eris, m., and vespera, -ae, f.,
    evening.
vespertinalis, -e, of the evening.
vestigium, -i, n., track, step.
vestimentum, -i, n., vestment.
vestio, 4, -ii, -itum, clothe.
vetustus, -a, -um, old.
vexo, 1, trouble.
vibro, 1, shake.

vices, defective, f., times.
vicinus, -a, -um, near by.
victrix, -icis, f., conqueress.
victrix, victorious.
vicus, -i, m., row of houses.
videlicet, namely, of course.
videor, 2, seem.
vigilia, -ae, f., vigil.
vilis, -e, cheap.
villa, -ae, f., town.
vincio, 4, -xi, -ctum, bind.
vindico, 1, claim, settle.
vinea, -ae, f., vine.
violo, 1, impair.
vipera, -ae, f., viper.
virga, -ae, f., branch, rod.
virgula, -ae, f., twig.
viridis, -e, active.
virilis, -e, manly.
vis, defective, f., force (pl. vires,
    strength).
visus, -us, sight.
vitis, -is, f., vine.
vitrum, -i, n., glass.
vivifico, 1, quicken to life.
vivus, -a, -um, living.
vocula, -ae, f., word.
volo, velle, volui, wish.
voluntas, -atis, f., will.
voluptas, -atis, f., pleasure.
votum, -i, n., prayer.
vox, vocis, f., voice.
vulgo, commonly.
vulgus, -i, n., common people.
vultus, -us, m., countenance.

xenium, -i, n., gift.